# EAT ATE

# GUY MIRABELLA
# EAT ATE

PHOTOGRAPHY BY EARL CARTER

CHRONICLE BOOKS

SAN FRANCISCO

for Johanne

let's go to Paris and never
come back

Library of Congress Cataloging-in-Publication Data
available.

ISBN 978-0-8118-7111-2

Manufactured in China.

Design and layout by Guy Mirabella and Dominic Hofstede
Photographs by Earl Carter
Additional photograph on page 1 by Charlotte Wilson
Card pictured on page 71 courtesy Love and Clutter
Food styling by Caroline Velik

The publisher would like to thank the following people
for their generosity in supplying props for the book:
Izzi & Popo, Manon bis, Cranfields, Bliink Interiors,
Minimax, Roost, Lyn Gardener and Empire Vintage.

10 9 8 7 6 5 4 3 2 1

Chronicle Books LLC
680 Second Street
San Francisco, California 94107

www.chroniclebooks.com

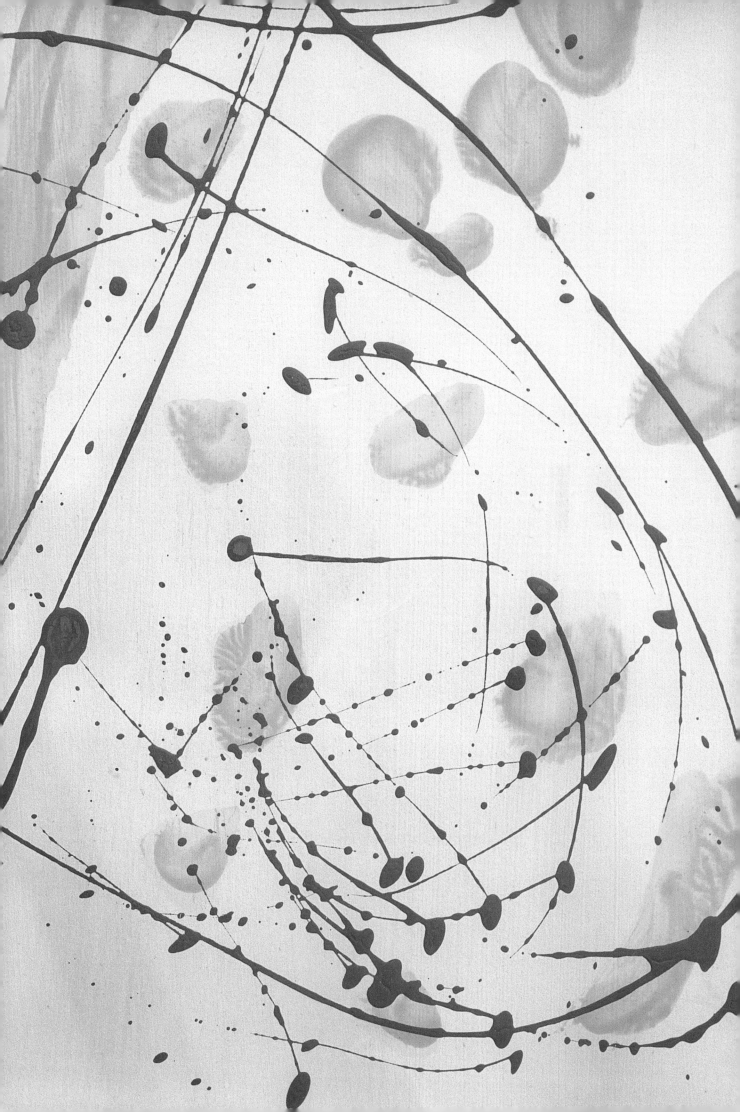

## Introduction

As a child, I lived on a small farm on the Mornington Peninsula in Victoria. We had geese, ducks, chickens, cows, horses, pigs, dogs—the usual cornucopia of *animale di campania*—and we were self-sufficient, growing our own fruit and vegetables. It made sense to eat what was in season with the succession of months bringing us the food we loved.

It was within the wooden slatted walls of our tiny farmhouse that my parents, Diego and Pina, united us in their "kingdom of Sicily." Mary, our Jersey cow, provided us with our daily milk. True to her Sicilian upbringing, my mother would heat Mary's milk, then pour it into bowls and add torn bread and a few drops of coffee. Then, because we were in Australia, Mum would break Teddy Bear biscuits over the top.

While other children were sent off to school with cheese and ham sandwiches for lunch, my mother would pack us fried onion and red pepper sandwiches made with thick slices of pasta dura bread that Dad bought from Victoria Market. Dad had a stall in the market and during the broccoli season Mum would fill our sandwiches with leftover broccoli fritti, just like the recipe on page 104. Lunch was eaten in the shelter shed, rain, hail or shine, and I enjoyed every mouthful.

I couldn't wait to get home after school to watch Mum preparing the evening meal and to eat her delicious food. My memories of being by her side, watching her and breathing in the aromas from the pots of bubbling *salsa di pomodoro* that she prepared, have had an enormous influence on how I cook and enjoy food as an adult.

In the center of our kitchen was a big, chunky wooden table where I would draw, paint and do my homework. In winter, Mum would toast bread over the fire for us, and spread it with butter and a sprinkle of sugar.

In summer, she would pour extra-virgin olive oil onto a flat plate with a little ground black pepper, into which we'd dip slices of grilled bread. Sometimes, Dad would bring in freshly picked, juicy tomatoes from the garden and squeeze the juices and flesh onto the bread.

My maternal grandparents were shepherds in Sicily. Mum left the island when she was nineteen to come to Australia to marry my father; they had been sweethearts since she was eleven and he was thirteen. Mum never saw her parents again. Dad's parents grew up, met and married in New York. They returned to their familial home, Calatafimi in Sicily, with their first two children, and the rest of their kids were born there in the village. With their American-accented English, Nonno and Nonna seemed more worldly than anyone I had ever met. They always walked straight and tall and spoke the truth.

I am also fortunate to have many uncles and aunts who love their food. Zia Franca's *arancini*. Zia Pipina's *cotoletta di vitella fritte*. Zia Vicenzina's olives and *dolci*. Zio Frank and Zia Maria's marinated eggplants and salted dried ricotta. Zia Marianna's biscotti. Comari and Compari Caleca's panettone. My Padrina Maria and Padrino Vince's seafood. The gorgeous marzipan fruit and sheep Zia Vittina would make at Easter and Christmas. My mother's brother, Zio Giovanni, who makes the best fennel and pork sausages.

Arrivederci a Venezia
Goodbye to Venice

My history and memories are built on the experiences I've shared at the table with my relatives. Their blood runs in my veins, along with that of the Phoenicians, Greeks, Byzantines, Arabs, Normans, Spaniards, the Bourbons of Naples and many others from around the Mediterranean who settled in Sicily.

Over the centuries, Italians have developed a diet that rejoices in the pleasures of good health and good eating. It is all about great produce and simple ingredients, carefully prepared without fuss.

I am not a trained chef; until just a few years ago, most of my working life had been spent as a book designer and teacher. But I was always restless, and after a few too many creative director positions gone wrong, I decided to try something different.

It had always been my dream to open a place like Shop Ate Café and Store. It has given me somewhere to cook and serve the style of food that I love to eat at home. A simple omelette with toasted sourdough, linguine with shaved zucchini, roasted pumpkin, lemon zest and crunchy hazelnuts, great coffee and excellent service.

For me, the café is the perfect way of bringing people together to share experiences and to provoke, love and challenge.

This book celebrates my Italian spirit, and also pays homage to the importance of family. When our children were growing up, my wife Johanne and I would sit down for dinner with them every night. Now, our favorite weekends are when all our children and their friends come to eat at our table.

Unlike traditional cookbooks, there are no starter, main meal and dessert chapters in this book. Rather, the recipes are organized according to the themes that give me the comfort and freedom to express the way I cook, eat, design and paint. Extravagance, generosity, love, tradition, life, food—it's all about truth, beauty and perseverance.

# /Extravagance
Generosity
Love
Tradition
Life
Food

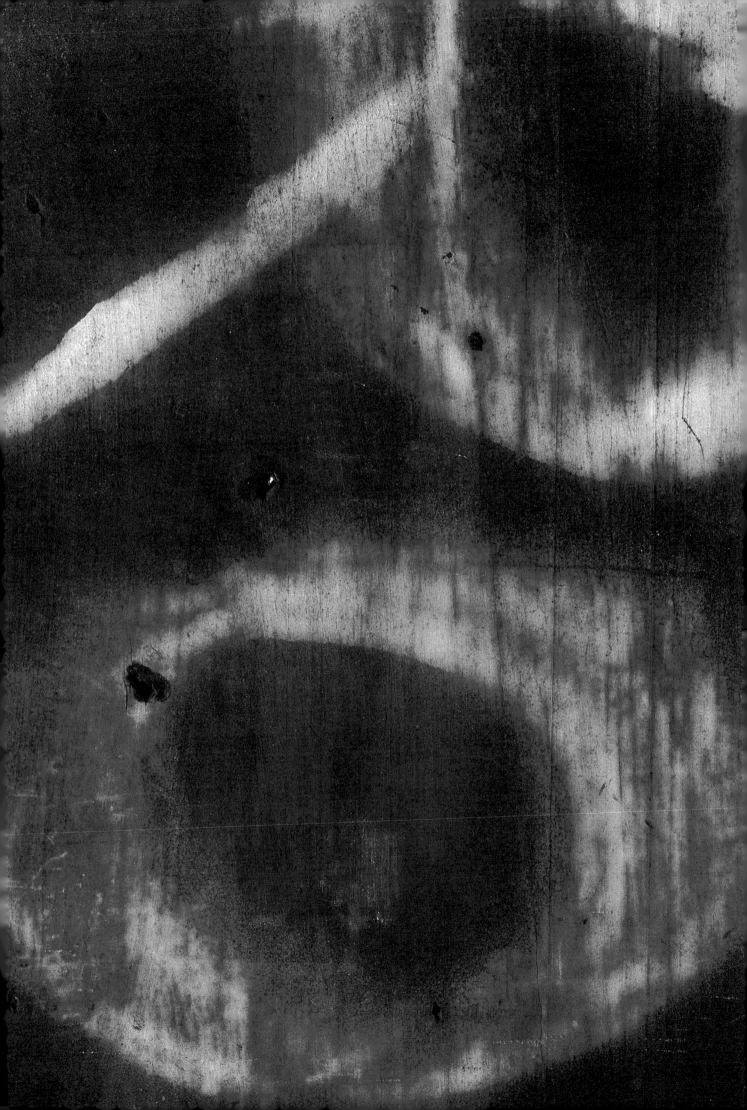

In the disappearing splendor of the aristocratic Sicily in Giuseppe Tomasi di Lampedusa's novel *The Leopard*, made into a movie by Luchino Visconti, old and new worlds collide. It is equally the story of a dying, extravagant lifestyle and the endorsement of progress. The characters' words and dusty kisses grasp at your heart as the life they know quietly slips away. In the first scenes of Martin Scorsese's film *The Age of Innocence*, the director takes his main character through a sequence of intensely decorated rooms in order to prepare him, and the viewer, for the ultimate destination of the ballroom. It takes Scorsese ten minutes of extravagance to prepare us for this ultimate flamboyance, and another ten minutes for it to play out. Similarly, Visconti builds up for an hour-and-a-half to get to *The Leopard*'s extraordinary banquet scene, which lasts for a glorious forty-five minutes.

However, my parents have taught me the *real* secret of extravagance: generosity. When you cook for people, don't be mean. Be hospitable; cook lovely, rich meals that are meant for special occasions, and serve an abundance of food. Always use great ingredients, preferably home-grown. Instead of using one variety of mushroom for a mushroom risotto, use three or four. A roast chicken, simply prepared and teamed with just a hint of extravagance, like muscatel grapes, becomes a memorable meal. Or keep it simple, and serve a large bowl of juicy, big, fresh purple figs with a shot of marsala.

# Egg, white anchovies and pancetta salad

Cumin, coriander, sesame seeds, hazelnuts—the words sound so lovely and warm on their own—but when ground together the spices become *dukkah*, a word that always reminds me of Al Pacino saying "Hooo-ahhh!" in the film *Scent of a Woman*. Teamed with perfectly cooked eggs, crisp peppery rocket, silky white anchovies from Sicily and freshly sliced smoky pancetta, it makes a delightful aromatic and extravagant celebration of Mediterranean and Middle Eastern flavors.

White anchovies are fillets marinated in vinegar and oil—they are more subtle than their salted counterparts, and have a fresh tang from the vinegar. You can find them in good delis.

Serves 4

4 slices day-old sourdough
8 slices mild pancetta
1 large red bell pepper
2 tablespoons extra-virgin olive oil
zest and juice of 1 small lemon
1 tablespoon white vinegar
4 eggs (or 8 quail eggs)
8 white anchovies

4 large handfuls of arugula
salt and freshly ground black pepper
handful of parsley
8 chives, cut into ¾-inch lengths
4 tarragon sprigs, leaves picked
1 tablespoon dukkah (available in Middle Eastern markets)

Preheat the oven to 400°F. Break the bread into bite-sized pieces and place on a tray. Bake the pieces, moving them around occasionally, for about 15 minutes or until golden. Tip them into a large bowl and then lay the pancetta slices on the tray and bake for about 10 minutes or until crisp.

Heat the grill of a barbecue or a chargrill pan and cook the bell pepper, turning it regularly, until blackened all over (you can also do this in the oven). Remove from the heat and let it cool a little, then peel off the skin and remove the stem and seeds. Cut or tear the flesh into thin strips.

For the dressing, combine the oil, lemon zest and juice in a jar with a lid and shake.

Fill a saucepan with around 2⅓ inches of water. Add the vinegar and bring the water to a gentle simmer. In a small bowl crack the first egg. Gently swirl the simmering water and slide the egg in. Repeat with the remaining eggs and poach them all for about 4 minutes, or until the whites have set but the yolks are still runny. Remove the eggs with a slotted spoon and set aside to drain. If using quail eggs, boil whole for 3 minutes.

Put the pancetta, bell pepper, anchovies and arugula into the bowl with the bread. Pour in the dressing and toss gently. Divide among serving plates and top each salad with an egg (or halved quail eggs). Sprinkle with the salt, pepper, herbs and dukkah and serve while the eggs are still warm.

# Marinated eye fillet, herb mascarpone, potato and pine nut salad

I get a lot of pleasure and learning from reading cookbooks, just as other folk read novels. One of my favorites is *The French Laundry Cookbook* by Thomas Keller. His method of tying the meat and seasoning it the day before it is cooked is a terrific piece of advice; the meat keeps its shape and the "salt has time to penetrate the flesh and intensify the flavor." The herb mascarpone and potato and pine nut salad add an aromatic herbiness and nutty crunch.

Serves 4

EYE FILLET
7 tablespoons olive oil, plus extra for frying
1 tablespoon white balsamic vinegar
3 garlic cloves, finely chopped
3–4 herb sprigs such as basil and
    parsley, chopped
four 7-ounce eye fillet steaks

HERB MASCARPONE
2 teaspoons horseradish cream
2 large tablespoons heavy cream
1 teaspoon wholegrain mustard
1 cup mascarpone
juice of ½ lemon
½ teaspoon white balsamic vinegar

1 tablespoon chopped chives
1 tablespoon chopped parsley
1 tablespoon chopped basil
1 tablespoon chopped chervil
salt and freshly ground black pepper

SALAD
1½ pounds potatoes, washed
salt
½ cup pine nuts, toasted
handful of parsley, chopped
¼ cup extra-virgin olive oil
1 teaspoon white balsamic vinegar
freshly ground black pepper

For the eye fillet: combine the 7 tablespoons oil, vinegar, garlic and herbs and rub the mixture into the steaks. Cover and place in the refrigerator to marinate for at least 5 hours or, ideally, overnight.

For the herb mascarpone: lightly whisk the horseradish, heavy cream, mustard, mascarpone, lemon juice and vinegar. Add the herbs and season with salt and pepper. Refrigerate until serving.

For the salad: cook the potatoes in a large pot of salted boiling water until tender. Drain and set aside until cool enough to touch, then peel and cut crosswise into slices about ½ inch thick. Place in a bowl and add the pine nuts and parsley. Combine the oil and vinegar and season with salt and pepper, then pour the mixture over the potatoes and gently toss. Leave the potatoes at room temperature until serving.

One hour before you want to cook the steaks, take them out of the fridge. When you are ready to cook them, preheat the oven to 350°F. Heat a barbecue, a chargrill pan, or a regular frying pan over medium–high heat and brush it with oil. Cook the steaks for about 2 minutes on each side, then roast on a tray for around 5 minutes for medium-rare, or until cooked to your liking. Cover the steaks with foil and rest in a warm spot for 15 minutes.

Spoon the potato salad into the center of 4 plates. Lay a steak on top and add a generous dollop of herb mascarpone, and serve.

# Chargrilled chili calamari and radicchio salad

Sweet, hot and bitter flavors combine to create the ultimate calamari starter for any dinner party. Alternatively, you can pile the salad onto a large serving platter, as I do, garnished with freshly cut, firm, bright green limes.

The calamari are best when they're around the size of a small hand, as they are most tender. You can serve this salad warm or at room temperature.

Serves 4

2 pounds whole calamari (several small young calamari rather than 1 large one is best)
3 small red chilies, finely chopped
zest and juice of 1 lemon
1 garlic clove, finely chopped
½ cup olive oil

salt and freshly ground black pepper
1 radicchio, tough outer leaves discarded
handful of basil leaves
½ pound cherry tomatoes, halved
1 tablespoon extra-virgin olive oil
lime wedges

Clean the calamari by taking the head and tentacles in a bunch in your hand and pulling them out of the body. Cut the head from the tentacles and discard (cut high enough so the tentacles remain attached in a cluster). Cut out the small beak from inside the tentacles (small calamari may not have one). Pull out the strip of transparent cartilage from inside the body and rinse the body and tentacles thoroughly. Pat everything dry.

Combine the calamari tentacles and bodies (the bodies should look like tubes with triangular wings attached) in a bowl with the chilies, lemon zest and juice, garlic and olive oil. Season well with salt and pepper and toss, making sure the marinade gets inside the tubes. Leave for 1 hour.

Heat the grill of a barbecue, a chargrill pan or a regular frying pan over high heat. Cook the calamari bodies and tentacles until lightly charred on all sides, then remove to a chopping board. Halve the tentacle clusters lengthwise, giving equal tentacles to each half. If the tentacles are very long you may also wish to cut them in half crosswise. Place in a mixing bowl. Slice the tubes into ⅛-inch rings, slicing through the wings as you go, and add everything to the bowl.

Break or tear up the radicchio leaves and add to the calamari along with the basil, tomatoes and extra-virgin olive oil. Toss and place on a serving platter. Serve with the lime wedges.

# Roast chicken, muscatels

Half the pleasure of this dish is getting your hands into it, rubbing the fresh herbs, lemon zest and juice under the skin and all over the outside of the bird to keep the meat moist and full of flavor. The other half is the gratification when the dish comes out of the oven, the golden brown of the chicken contrasting with the rustic dark colors of the grapes, combined with the squishy texture of tomatoes. Sigh deeply and be rewarded as you set it on the table, for the best bit of all is in the eating.

Serves 8

two 3-pound free-range chickens
zest and juice of 1 lemon
salt and freshly ground black pepper
small bunch sage, leaves picked
small bunch thyme, leaves picked
4 garlic cloves, crushed
1 cup butter, softened

½ cup olive oil
1 pound bunch muscatel grapes, separated
    into small clusters
8 ripe tomatoes (with their stems attached
    if desired)
2 cups dry white wine
handful of rosemary sprigs

Preheat the oven to 400°F. Wash the chickens inside and out and pat them dry with paper towel. Trim away any excess fat.

Place a chicken on its breast and use kitchen scissors to cut along each side of the backbone and remove it. Turn the chicken over so the breast is facing up and gently press down on it with the palm of your hand to crack the breastbone. Starting near the neck, gently insert your fingers under the skin and gradually push your fingers through to separate the skin from the breast and thigh meat. The skin should remain attached but loosened. Repeat with the other chicken.

Rub the lemon zest, salt and pepper beneath the skin of the chickens, inside the cavities and all over the outside. Squeeze the lemon juice under the skin, into the cavities and over the outside too. Follow by rubbing in the sage and thyme, garlic and half the butter so all surfaces are well coated.

Pour the oil into a large roasting tray. Put the grape clusters (including stems) and tomatoes in the tray and crush them lightly with the back of a spoon. Place the chickens on top, breast-side down, then pour in half the wine. Roast in the oven for about 30 minutes, then turn the birds over and baste with pan juices and sprinkle with the rosemary sprigs. Roast for another 40 minutes, until golden brown.

Remove the chickens, grapes and tomatoes from the tray and place on a warm serving platter. Cover with foil. Add the remaining butter and wine to the tray and place it on the stove over high heat. Scrape the residue from the sides and bottom of the tray and simmer the sauce until it has thickened slightly. Pour it over the chickens and serve.

# Chicken ragù, zucchini and macadamias

This is a gorgeous, robust way of cooking chicken, with fragrant herbs, fruity vincotto and wine to add some lusciousness. It's finger-licking stuff, and so easy to make. The preparation can be done way in advance and then you can just leave the ragù on the stove to gently cook away. And to accompany the chicken there's an effortlessly easy zucchini side dish that I put together as an afterthought. I was surprised to discover how the flavors went so well with the ragù, and it's also terrific with Middle Eastern or Mediterranean dishes.

Serves 4

⅓ cup olive oil, plus 1 tablespoon
3 pounds free-range chicken, cut into 8 pieces
1 medium onion, finely chopped
1 medium carrot, finely chopped
1 celery stick, finely chopped
pinch of dried chili flakes (optional)
2 garlic cloves, finely sliced
4 slices prosciutto, roughly chopped
2 dill sprigs, roughly chopped
3–4 parsley sprigs, roughly chopped,
    plus small handful of parsley
2 rosemary sprigs, leaves picked
4 sage leaves

1 bay leaf
3 thyme sprigs
grated zest of 1 lemon
salt and freshly ground black pepper
½ cup vincotto (available in gourmet markets)
2 cups dry white wine
2 cups chicken stock

3 small zucchini, thinly sliced lengthwise
½ cup currants
1 cup macadamias, chopped

2 spring onions, finely sliced

Heat the ⅓ cup oil in a large heavy-based saucepan over medium heat. Add the chicken pieces and brown them all over. Add the onion, carrot, celery and chili (if using) and cook, stirring occasionally, until the onion is translucent. Add the garlic, prosciutto, herbs and lemon zest and season with salt and pepper. Continue cooking for about 10 minutes. Add the vincotto, wine and stock and cook uncovered for about 45 minutes. If you find the liquid evaporates too quickly, add another 1 cup of stock or water.

When the chicken is almost ready, prepare the zucchini. Heat the 1 tablespoon oil in a large frying pan and add the zucchini, currants and nuts. Fry, stirring occasionally, for 5–10 minutes or until the zucchini starts to turn golden brown. Transfer to a serving bowl. Ladle the chicken into a separate dish and garnish with the handful of parsley and spring onions.

# Roast beef, olive, tomato and oregano stuffing with crushed potatoes

My parents have always used crushed garlic and basil as a stuffing. They also use basil and garlic as a paste for brushing on meat or fish when barbecuing, or as an intense, but simple pasta sauce. For more intense flavors with this dish you can marinate the beef for twenty-four hours and then bring it back to room temperature before cooking.

Crushed potatoes are best crushed and dressed while they're still hot, so they absorb all the oil, and make sure you season with lots of freshly ground pepper.

Serves 4

one 2-pound piece scotch fillet
    (or rib-eye roast)

STUFFING
2 garlic cloves, peeled
1 medium bunch basil, leaves picked
¼ teaspoon salt
2 pounds ripe tomatoes, skinned, seeded
    and roughly chopped
5 oregano sprigs, leaves picked
¼ cup olive oil
½ cup green olives, pitted and sliced
½ cup black olives, pitted and sliced
freshly ground black pepper
1 cup grated grana padano

POTATOES
12 medium red potatoes, washed
salt
½ cup extra-virgin olive oil
handful of parsley
1 small red onion, finely sliced
1 tablespoon small capers, rinsed
1 tablespoon dukkah (available in
    Middle Eastern markets)
freshly ground black pepper

Trim the meat of any fat, then make a cut lengthwise along the longest side of the fillet so it can be opened out flat and stuffed.

For the stuffing: pound the garlic, basil and salt to a rough paste using a mortar and pestle. Transfer to a mixing bowl and add the tomatoes, oregano, oil and olives. Season with pepper and taste to see if the mixture needs any more salt.

Open the beef flat and spread on most of the stuffing. Sprinkle with the grana padano. Roll the beef around the stuffing and tie with string to hold it in a tight cylinder. Place the beef in an ovenproof skillet and rub the outside of the meat with the remaining stuffing. Leave to marinate at room temperature for 1 hour.

Preheat the oven to 400°F. Put the skillet on the stove over medium heat and sear the meat on all sides. This will take about 3–4 minutes. Transfer the skillet to the oven and bake for 35–40 minutes, which should cook the meat medium-rare, but cook it for longer if you wish. Cover the meat with foil and leave to rest in a warm place for 30 minutes.

For the potatoes: cook the potatoes in a large pot of salted boiling water until tender, then drain. Without peeling them, lightly crush the potatoes with a masher and place in a serving bowl. Add the remaining ingredients and season with salt and pepper. Gently toss everything together.

Cut the string from the beef, slice into portions and serve on warm plates with the potatoes.

# Mushroom risotto

This risotto combines various types of mushrooms. If you are lucky enough to pick some exquisite pine mushrooms, you'll find they add real elegance. My son, Paul, was cooking this risotto one night and he used just a touch of vermouth instead of wine. The vermouth adds a gentility to this dish that I love.

Serves 4

5 cups chicken or vegetable stock, or water
¼ cup olive oil
5 tablespoons butter
1 medium onion, finely chopped
1 carrot, finely chopped
1 celery stick, finely chopped
pinch of dried chili flakes (optional)
2 garlic cloves, finely chopped
7 ounces cremini mushrooms, halved or quartered

⅓ pound oyster mushrooms, halved
1½ cups carnaroli rice
¼ cup vermouth
¼ pound enoki mushrooms, ends trimmed
1 medium bunch parsley, finely chopped
3 thyme sprigs, leaves picked
zest and juice of 1 lemon
1 cup grated grana padano, plus extra to serve
salt and freshly ground black pepper

Pour the stock into a saucepan and bring to a simmer. Meanwhile, heat the oil and 4 tablespoons of butter in a second heavy-based saucepan. Add the onion, carrot, celery and chili (if using) and cook until the onion is translucent. Add the garlic and cook for 30 seconds without browning. Add the cremini and oyster mushrooms and cook gently, stirring occasionally, until they start to turn golden brown. Add the rice and continue stirring for 2 minutes. Add the vermouth and stir until it evaporates, then add a ladleful of the simmering stock and stir until absorbed. Keep adding liquid gradually in this way for 15–18 minutes.

Taste the risotto—the rice should be firm to the bite. If you prefer, cook for another 3–5 minutes, but no more, until the rice is tender in the middle but not completely soft.

Remove the risotto from the heat and add the enoki mushrooms, parsley, thyme, lemon zest and juice, grana padano and remaining tablespoon of butter. Season with salt and pepper. Stir the ingredients through and then cover and rest for 2 minutes. Serve in warm bowls with extra grana padano on top.

# Ocean trout, citrus, mango and peach salad

This salad is all about fresh, simply prepared ingredients coming together with no fuss. Don't be put off by the long ingredients list. Take each step and fragrant ingredient as it comes, and in no time you will be back the sun, enjoying the summer weather.

Serves 12

DRESSING
1 bunch coriander, roots and stems
    washed and roughly chopped
    (leaves reserved for the salad)
2 garlic cloves, peeled
2 small red chilies, roughly chopped
1½-inch piece ginger, peeled and
    finely chopped
1 lemongrass stalk (white part only),
    finely chopped
pinch of salt
1 tablespoon dried shrimp
1 tablespoon fish sauce
zest and juice of 2 limes
1 tablespoon superfine sugar
2 tablespoons olive oil
2 tablespoons water

SALAD
2 oranges
3 green mangoes
3 unripe peaches
½ Chinese cabbage, finely sliced
¼ red cabbage, finely sliced

1 carrot, cut into matchsticks1 cucumber,
halved lengthwise, seeded
and cut into matchsticks
1 red bell pepper, cut into matchsticks
1 small red onion, finely sliced
4 radishes, cut into wafer-thin slices
handful of bean shoots
¼ pound baby pea shoots
1 bunch watercress, leaves picked
½ bunch Vietnamese mint, leaves picked
½ bunch Thai basil, leaves picked
3 spring onions, finely sliced diagonally
    (reserve some to garnish)
½ bunch chives, chopped (reserve some
    to garnish)

FISH
2 tablespoons olive oil
six 4-ounce ocean trout fillets, pin bones
    removed with tweezers

salt and freshly ground black pepper
½ cup peanuts or hazelnuts, toasted
    and chopped

For the dressing: pound the coriander roots and stems, garlic, chilies, ginger, lemongrass and salt to a paste using a mortar and pestle. Roughly pound in the shrimp. Add the fish sauce, lime zest and juice, sugar, olive oil and water, stirring until the sugar dissolves. Set aside.
*Continued*

# Ocean trout, citrus, mango and peach salad (continued)

For the salad: cut the peel from the oranges, then cut out the segments and place in a large bowl. Cut the peel from the mangoes, then slice off the cheeks. Lay the cheeks flat and slice crosswise into thin half-moons. Cut away any mango flesh still attached to the stone and slice similarly. Add the mango to the bowl. Stone the peaches, slice into more half-moons and add. Put all remaining ingredients in the bowl, including the coriander leaves reserved from the dressing, and gently toss everything together. If you are preparing the dish in advance, cover this undressed salad and refrigerate.

For the fish: heat the oil in a frying pan over medium heat and add the fillets skin-side down. Cook for 6–8 minutes, then turn the fish and take the pan off the heat, covering it with a lid. Leave for 2–3 minutes, then take the fish out of the pan to cool. When cool enough to handle, remove the skin and discard it, and shred the flesh with your fingers.

To serve, add the dressing and fish to the salad and season with salt and pepper. Gently toss the salad and tip onto a large platter. Sprinkle with the nuts, reserved spring onions and reserved chives.

# Asparagus, gorgonzola and lemon risotto

Gorgonzola adds a lovely creaminess to this risotto – not that it really needs it, but it can't hurt, and it's delicious!

Serves 4

1⅓ quarts water

salt

12 asparagus spears, ends trimmed,
    stalks cut diagonally into 1-inch pieces

2 tablespoons olive oil

4 tablespoons butter

1 medium onion, finely chopped

1 medium carrot, finely chopped

1 celery stick, finely chopped

2 garlic cloves, finely chopped

1 small red chili, finely chopped

1 cup dry white wine

1½ cups arborio rice

1 cup milk

1 cup grated pecorino

3 ounces gorgonzola, cut into ½-inch cubes

2 cups grated grana padano

zest and juice of 1 lemon

large handful of arugula

salt and freshly ground black pepper

Bring the water to boil in a saucepan, adding some salt. Add the asparagus and cook for 3–4 minutes. Remove with a slotted spoon to a bowl of cold water with ice cubes in it so the asparagus remains emerald green. Keep the cooking water simmering.

Heat the oil and half the butter in a heavy-based saucepan. Add the onion, carrot and celery and cook until the onion is translucent. Add the garlic and chili and cook for 30 seconds without letting the garlic brown. Add the wine to the pan and simmer until it has reduced by half. Add the rice and stir for 2 minutes.

Add a ladleful of asparagus water and stir until absorbed. Continue adding water in this way for 15–18 minutes—by then the rice should be cooked but still firm to the bite. If you prefer, cook for another 3–5 minutes, but no more, until the rice is tender in the middle but not completely soft.

Just before the rice is ready, gently heat the milk, pecorino and gorgonzola in a saucepan until the cheeses melt and add this to the risotto with the asparagus. Stir until the asparagus is warm.

Remove the risotto from the heat and add the remaining butter as well as the grana padano, lemon zest and juice and arugula. Season with salt and pepper. Stir the ingredients through and then cover and rest the risotto for 2 minutes. Serve in warm bowls.

# Artichoke, radicchio, tomato and chicken liver risotto

Four of my favorite things come together in this recipe, and I'm especially fond of artichokes. Cooking the risotto with the artichoke water intensifies the flavor. This gives it a sweetness that is balanced by the slight bitterness of the radicchio and made more luxurious and earthy with the addition of chicken livers. If you like, you can omit the chicken livers and serve it as a vegetarian risotto or as an accompaniment to other dishes. This method of cooking artichokes is great for other kinds of artichoke dishes as well.

Serves 6

5 cups water

1 lemon, cut in half

6 artichokes

½ cup olive oil

1 pound ripe tomatoes, skinned, seeded and roughly chopped

2 garlic cloves, finely sliced

2 tablespoons finely chopped parsley

2–3 rosemary sprigs, leaves chopped

salt and freshly ground black pepper

4 tablespoons butter

1 medium onion, finely chopped

1 medium leek (white part only), finely sliced

1 medium carrot, finely chopped

1 celery stick, finely chopped

½ pound chicken livers, trimmed of fat and halved

1 cup dry white wine

1 ½ cups arborio rice

2 cups grated grana padano

1 radicchio, large leaves torn into pieces

Put the water and the juice of one lemon half in a saucepan. Cut off the lower stem of each artichoke, leaving about 2 inches attached to the head. Peel away several layers of leaves until you reach the pale inner leaves. Cut off the top about 1 inch down, then cut into quarters lengthwise. Scrape off the fragments of hairy choke from each quarter using the tip of a knife, rub all the cut surfaces with the remaining lemon half and drop both lemon pieces into the saucepan.

Put a few handfuls of artichoke off-cuts and leaves into the saucepan with the artichoke quarters and bring to a boil, then cover and simmer for 10 minutes. Strain the water into a container, then pour the water back into the pot. Pick out the artichoke quarters and discard the leaves.

Preheat the oven to 350°F. Brush a tray with 2 tablespoons of the oil and add the artichoke quarters, tomatoes, garlic, parsley and rosemary. Season with salt and pepper and mix together. Roast for about 20 minutes.

Meanwhile, bring the artichoke water back to a simmer. Heat the remaining oil and half the butter in another heavy-based saucepan. Add the onion, leek, carrot and celery and cook until the onion is translucent. Add the livers and cook, stirring, for 3–4 minutes until browned all over. Spoon them onto a plate and keep warm.

Add the wine to the onion mixture, scraping any residue from the bottom of the pan. Simmer until reduced by half, then add the rice and stir for 2 minutes. Add a ladleful of artichoke water and stir until absorbed, adding water in this way for 15–18 minutes. Taste the risotto—the rice should be firm to the bite.

Turn off the heat and add the rest of the butter and the grana padano. Season with salt and pepper. Add the hot artichoke and tomato mixture, the livers and the radicchio and stir again. Leave to rest for 2 minutes, then serve in warm bowls.

# Fig cake, marsala figs

As a child, when my parents' friends came to visit I can remember big bowls of ripe purple figs being passed around with short glasses of sweet Sicilian marsala. These days I prefer my marsala dry but my figs still ripe and juicy.

A customer came into the café one day carrying a basket lined with fig leaves and overflowing with unwanted purple fruit. This cake came about thanks to Moira's abundance of beautiful figs.

Serves 8

1 ¼ cups self-rising flour
¾ cup superfine sugar
⅔ cup butter, softened
1 teaspoon vanilla extract
3 eggs
1 apple, peeled and grated
8 ripe figs, halved
confectioners' sugar

MARSALA FIGS
1 ¼ cups water
1 ½ cups sugar
8 ripe figs, halved
⅓ cup dry marsala

whipped cream

Preheat the oven to 350°F. Butter a 13-by-9-inch baking dish and line the base with parchment paper.

In a mixing bowl, beat the flour, sugar, butter, vanilla and eggs with electric beaters for 3–4 minutes, until the mixture becomes pale. Fold in the apple, then scoop the mixture into the baking dish. Dot the fig halves (cut-side up) over the top of the batter and bake in the oven for 25–30 minutes or until golden brown. Remove from the oven and let cool.

For the marsala figs: heat the water and sugar in a saucepan until the sugar dissolves. Add the figs and marsala and simmer gently for 10 minutes.

Dust the cake with confectioners' sugar and serve warm or at room temperature cut into squares. Spoon the marsala figs and plenty of whipped cream on the side.

# Tiramisù, my way

This dessert's name comes from the Italian morning ritual of going into a café and asking the bartender for a *tiramisù*—something to "pick me up." A shot of rich, thick Vov, made from eggs, sugar and marsala, is poured, which gives the drinker energy.

The "my way" in the title refers to the fact that the only way to eat tiramisù is for breakfast. It is the only thing you need and it really does pick you up! In Italy, dessert is always enjoyed best when eaten at breakfast.

Serves 8–12

3 cups freshly brewed black coffee
2⅓ tablespoons sugar
⅓ cup brandy
6 eggs, separated

1⅓ cups mascarpone
Dutch cocoa
30 lady fingers

Combine the coffee, 1 teaspoon of the sugar and the brandy in a wide bowl and set aside to cool.

Place the egg yolks in a bowl that will fit comfortably over a saucepan of simmering water. Off the heat, beat the yolks and the remaining sugar with electric beaters for about 5 minutes, until pale and creamy. Place the bowl over the pan of simmering water and continue beating for another 3 minutes, or until the mixture doubles in volume. Remove the bowl from the heat and beat a little longer, until the custard cools slightly. Set aside to cool completely, then add the mascarpone, stirring until smooth. In a separate bowl, beat the egg whites until they hold stiff peaks, then gently fold them into the custard.

Lightly dust the base of a bowl, dish or glasses with cocoa. Soak half the lady fingers in the coffee one at a time until they are well moistened but not too soft and lay them in the base of the bowl. Dust the biscuits with more cocoa, then spread half the custard on top. Add another layer of moistened lady fingers and cocoa, then top with the rest of the custard and a final dusting of cocoa. Cover and refrigerate for at least 5 hours.

Cut or spoon the tiramisù onto serving plates, dusting with more cocoa if you wish.

# Macadamia and Grand Marnier orange cake, mascarpone

The hit of liqueur in this cake always reminds me of those black-and-white Hollywood movies of the '40s and '50s that I can remember watching on television as a child. They always seemed to be set in hip places called the Rainbow Room or the Pink Pelican—names that to me were just as exotic as the liqueur.

Serves 8

1 cup butter, softened
¾ cup superfine sugar
pinch of salt
5 eggs
1 pear, cored and diced, or 1 apple, peeled,
    cored and diced
1 cup macadamias, roughly chopped
grated zest of 1 orange
½ cup freshly squeezed orange juice, strained
½ cup Grand Marnier
1½ cup self-rising flour

SYRUP
⅔ cup sugar
½ cup freshly squeezed orange juice, strained
1 tablespoon Grand Marnier

MASCARPONE
1 pound mascarpone
1 tablespoon superfine sugar
2 tablespoons Grand Marnier

Preheat the oven to 350°F. Butter a 9-inch round cake pan and line the base and sides with parchment paper.

Cream the butter, sugar and salt with electric beaters for about 5 minutes, until pale and fluffy. Beat in the eggs one at a time, beating well after each addition. Add the pear, macadamias and orange zest, then add the liquids and flour alternately, mixing gently until well combined.

Spoon the batter into the prepared pan and bake for about 45 minutes, or until the top is golden and the cake tests done with a skewer.

For the syrup: combine the ingredients in a saucepan and heat until the sugar dissolves. Prick small holes in the cake with the skewer and pour over the syrup. Let the cake cool in the pan.

For the mascarpone: combine the mascarpone, sugar and Grand Marnier in a bowl and stir until smooth. Transfer the cake to a plate, cut into slices and serve the mascarpone on the side. Alternatively, spread the mascarpone over the top of the cake.

# Panettone, raspberry sauce, drunken dates

This recipe was originally called Panettone with Summer Fruit and Nuts, but I love its new title, which includes drunken dates. It started off as a summer version of bread and butter pudding, but with a few changes here and there, and served on a platter for a buffet, it became a sort of deconstructed tower with the power to seduce even the slightest of sweet tooths.

Serves 8

RASPBERRY SAUCE
1 pound raspberries
juice of 1 lemon
2 tablespoons confectioners' sugar

1 cup pitted dates, halved lengthwise
1 cup raisins
1 cup brandy
1 pound mascarpone
1 cup cream

grated zest of 1 orange
½ cup dry marsala
8 ripe figs, halved
2 tablespoons rosewater
6 tablespoons superfine sugar
one 2-pound panettone
½ pound raspberries
1 cup flaked almonds, toasted
½ cup hazelnuts, toasted and chopped

For the sauce: purée the ingredients in a food processor or blender. Pass the mixture through a fine sieve to remove the seeds. This sauce can be made up to 3 days in advance (the fruit will start to separate from the sugar if left for much longer). Whisk the sauce again just before serving.

Combine the dates, raisins and brandy in a small saucepan and simmer until the liquid is absorbed and the fruit is plump. Set aside to cool.

Combine the mascarpone, cream, orange zest and 1 tablespoon of the marsala in a bowl and stir well. Set aside.

Place the figs cut-side up in a wide dish. Pour the rosewater over the figs and sprinkle with 1 tablespoon of the superfine sugar. Place them under a grill and cook until they caramelize.

Cut the panettone into 8 wedges. Brush the cut sides with the remaining marsala and sprinkle with the rest of the superfine sugar. Grill the wedges under medium heat until toasted and caramelized on both sides.

Serve the warm panettone wedges with a dollop of the mascarpone cream. Scatter with the dates and raisins, figs, raspberries and nuts and drizzle with the raspberry sauce.

# Hazelnut meringue cake, Galliano-soaked cranberries

What a happy time I have making this cake! Raspberries or strawberries are the fruit I usually stir through the cream, but when I was looking for something new recently I discovered some dried cranberries hidden away in a drawer. I soaked them in Galliano, which has a lovely flavor whispering of licorice and aniseed.

Serves 8–10

1 cup dried cranberries
2½ cups Galliano
1⅜ cups superfine sugar
8 egg whites
pinch of salt

1 cup hazelnut meal
1 cup hazelnuts, roughly chopped
1¼ cups cream
1½ pound ricotta
confectioners' sugar

Put the cranberries in a bowl with the Galliano and leave to soften.

Preheat the oven to 350°F. Line three large trays (pizza trays work well) with sheets of parchment paper. Trace the shape of a dinner plate (about 9 inches diameter) onto each sheet and spray the paper with oil spray. Sprinkle a tablespoon of the superfine sugar inside each circle and spread evenly.

Combine the egg whites, salt and remaining sugar (reserving 2 tablespoons) in a large bowl and beat with electric beaters for about 6 minutes, until firm and glossy. Gently fold in the hazelnut meal and spread the mixture over the sugar circles. Smooth and level out the tops, then sprinkle with the chopped hazelnuts. Bake in the oven for 25 minutes or until lightly browned, then remove from the oven and set aside to cool completely.

Whip the cream, ricotta and remaining 2 tablespoons of sugar until thick. Fold in the cranberries and any Galliano left in the bowl, reserving a tablespoon of cranberries to serve.

Place one layer of meringue on a serving plate and top with cranberry cream. Place a second meringue on top and add the rest of the cream. Add the last meringue, dust the top with confectioners' sugar and dot with cranberries.

Extravagance
/ Generosity
Love
Tradition
Life
Food

When cooking for others, generous cooks always prepare the food they themselves love to eat. It doesn't necessarily mean providing an abundance of food. Rather, it's all about cooking with the freshest, best-quality produce available. Bring out your favorite extra-virgin olive oil. Source ripe, juicy, just-picked tomatoes. At the market, look for fish with shiny, jewel-like eyes. And serve the apricots you picked, pale orange, slightly furry, squishy and warm, as you stood there under the tree, clinging to the past and thinking of tomorrow.

Generosity has no ego; it has nothing to do with your culture or nationality. Generosity is about respect, working together, trusting each other and sharing experiences in order to celebrate life. It has nothing to do with how you plate a dish, grate a tomato or what spice you use. Generosity has no time for indecisiveness.

Generosity is calm and thoughtful. It is about good taste, delicacy, good manners and the ability to surprise and listen. It is opening your arms, heart and head.

At the end of Dirk Bogarde's autobiography, *An Orderly Man*, he writes, "I can't help feeling that it is all going to be a tremendously exciting adventure, but I shall not let it go to my head. I'm an orderly man. Often pinched by doubt . . ."

—
There is a picnic
from my childhood that
I will always remember.
I was thirteen, and as my
father's car swayed along
the gravel road that led
to his cousin's house,
the countryside opened
up before us.
—

The wooden gates to the property were open, and behind them we could see a procession of children, women and men carrying platters and baskets covered with checkered towels. Those with free arms waved at us to follow them.

After traipsing through the long grass, we reached a spot with a creek running through it. Blankets were unpacked and shaken out, falling like hills on the pale green grass. The blankets were then covered with crisp linen cloths that looked like clouds. Big white bowls of salads were placed in the center, along with platters of roasted quail and chicken, frittata and arancini. There were freshly baked loaves of flat bread, some topped with anchovies, some with olives or zucchini, caramelized onions, squashed tomatoes and basil.

Somewhere close by, a fire had been lit and the smell of sardines roasting above hot orange coals wafted over. The aroma made us swallow deeply and our mouths water at the thought of their sweet flesh.

After that long lunch the day grew hot, and some of the men removed their shirts. They rubbed their stomachs slowly as they told jokes and stories, drinking wine from bottles with no labels. Groups of couples seated in the shade were playing cards, winning and losing. Shrieks of laughter rang through the air.

Children lay on their backs with eyes closed, lost in a world of their own as they journeyed to lands that only they could visit. Others were knee-deep in water, slowly inching their toes through the mud at the bottom of the creek.

The sounds grew quieter as the warm afternoon air wrapped around us. Later, platters of cannoli were brought out, piled upon each other and pointing in all directions, accompanied by strong black coffee.

The memory of this happy picnic is never far away from my thoughts. I hope I've captured its resonance at my café. I want my customers to feel at home there, and to embrace the simply prepared fresh food that we serve every day.

The conversation and ideas that I share with our regular customers are moments I treasure and recall when I feel exhausted at the end of another long day. The swapping of recipes, the best place to purchase ingredients or where to pick the best mushrooms (usually along the pine trees near the old Mooradooc train station just off the Nepean Highway, but don't tell anyone). The stories of people's families, what their children are doing. Watching some of our regulars courting, getting married and then walking in with baby buggies holding newborn children. We have lost count with the number of babies that have grown with us over the last six years. A few of them enter our kitchen as if it were their own. I love that confidence and honesty that children embrace. The stories that they have to tell and get out quickly and loudly with no time for breathing. Then there are a few brave souls who also enter our kitchen for the latest gossip and news around town. Their stories and excitement feed us, and for me it is an honor and a pleasure to be a part of their lives and their community. I love going to my little café every morning, it is the best place to be.

—

# Baked mushrooms, broken bread

This recipe was inspired by Mariapaola Dettore's recipe for *Funci 'ncartati* (mushrooms cooked in foil packages) from her book *Sicily*. It comes from the Agrigento area where mushrooms, wrapped in moistened butcher's paper, would be buried in the hot ashes in the fireplace to cook or placed on a grill above the glowing embers.

Serves 4

½ cup grated pepper pecorino
¼ cup fresh breadcrumbs
1 garlic clove, finely chopped
1 tablespoon finely chopped parsley,
    plus extra to serve
1 teaspoon finely chopped rosemary
    leaves, plus extra to serve
1 tablespoon thyme leaves, plus extra
    to serve

zest and juice of 1 small lemon
2 anchovies, chopped
⅓ cup olive oil, plus 2 tablespoons extra
splash of brandy
1 pound small-to-medium cremini mushrooms
salt and freshly ground black pepper
½ loaf ciabatta

In a bowl combine the pecorino, breadcrumbs, garlic, herbs and lemon zest. In another large bowl combine the lemon juice, anchovies, ⅓ cup oil, brandy and mushrooms and toss gently. Season with salt and pepper and toss again. Add the cheese and herb mixture and toss once more.

Preheat the oven to 400°F. Tip the mushroom mixture onto a large, lightly oiled baking sheet. Cover the sheet with foil so there are no gaps. Bake in the oven for 30 minutes then remove the foil and bake for another 15 minutes.

Meanwhile, tear the bread into bite-sized pieces and put onto another baking sheet. Toss with the 2 tablespoons oil and lots of pepper. Put the baking sheet in the oven with the mushrooms for the last 15 minutes, or until the bread is golden and crisp on the outside (but still a little soft in the middle).

To serve, put the bread on a large platter and spread the mushrooms and their juices over the top. Sprinkle with more parsley, rosemary and thyme.

# Chargrilled calamari, fennel and Asian herb salad

This recipe calls for what Italians call a "male" fennel, which is long, narrow and slightly bitter compared to the more bulbous "female" fennel. I grew up eating this type of fennel, as my father grew it in his garden, and we all seemed to prefer the bitter taste. The fennel in this dish gives the lovely sweet herbs a bit of a kick and it interacts beautifully with the other ingredients.

Serves 4

1 ⅓ pounds whole calamari (several small young calamari rather than 1 large one is best)
½ cup olive oil
salt and freshly ground black pepper
1-inch piece ginger, peeled and grated
2 small red chilies, thinly sliced lengthwise
½ pound cherry tomatoes, halved
1 medium "male" fennel bulb, thinly sliced

2 handfuls of bean shoots
½ bunch chives, cut into 1-inch lengths
handful of coriander leaves
handful of Vietnamese mint leaves
handful of Thai basil leaves
1 garlic clove, crushed
1 teaspoon superfine sugar
zest and juice of 2 limes
1 teaspoon fish sauce

Clean the calamari by taking the head and tentacles in a bunch in your hand and pulling them out of the body. Cut the head from the tentacles and discard (cut high enough so the tentacles remain attached in a cluster). Cut out the small beak from inside the tentacles (small calamari may not have one). Pull out the strip of transparent cartilage from inside the body and rinse the body and tentacles thoroughly. Pat everything dry.

Combine the calamari tentacles and bodies (the bodies should look like tubes with triangular wings attached) in a bowl with 2 tablespoons of the olive oil and season with salt and pepper.

Heat the grill of a barbecue, a chargrill pan or a regular frying pan over high heat. Cook the calamari bodies and tentacles until lightly charred on all sides, then remove to a chopping board. Halve the tentacle clusters lengthwise, giving equal tentacles to each half. If the tentacles are very long you may also wish to cut them in half crosswise. Place in a mixing bowl. Slice the tubes into ⅛-inch rings, slicing through the wings as you go, and add everything to the bowl.

Add the ginger, chilies, cherry tomatoes, fennel, bean shoots and herbs. In a jar combine the garlic, sugar, lime zest and juice, fish sauce and remaining oil. Shake well. Pour the dressing over the salad and gently toss everything together. Serve on a large platter.

# Chargrilled swordfish, roast potatoes and bell peppers, cherry tomatoes

Sicilians love their seafood. That's why you'll bump into them on piers all over Australia with squid jiggers, lines at the ready and the endless patience that seems to escape me. Maybe I'm not a true Sicilian after all, or maybe I'm just not a fisherman, but I do love seafood.

This dish was created to celebrate the richness and influence of Arabic flavors. If you would like to use more capers, go ahead, but be careful as they can be quite salty.

Serves 4

1 small red chili, finely chopped
1 tablespoon small capers, rinsed and
   chopped
1 teaspoon fennel seeds
2 tablespoons olive oil, plus extra for cooking
juice of 1 lemon
⅓ cup vincotto (available at gourmet markets)
salt and freshly ground black pepper
four ½-pound swordfish steaks

ROAST POTATOES AND BELL PEPPERS
1 pound red potatoes, peeled
salt
⅓ cup olive oil
1 large onion, finely sliced

3 large ripe tomatoes, skinned, seeded
   and chopped
1 garlic clove, finely chopped
1 red bell pepper, cut into strips
1 yellow bell pepper, cut into strips
1 celery stick, sliced diagonally
2 oregano sprigs, leaves picked
freshly ground black pepper

CHERRY TOMATOES
½ pound trussed cherry tomatoes
1 tablespoon olive oil
1 garlic clove, finely chopped
handful of parsley leaves
salt and freshly ground black pepper

Combine the chili, capers, fennel seeds, oil, lemon juice and vincotto in a wide bowl and season with salt and pepper. Add the swordfish steaks and rub them in the marinade. Leave for about 1 hour.

For the potatoes and bell peppers: cook the potatoes in a large pot of salted boiling water until just tender. Drain and cool a little, then cut them into ⅓-inch slices.

Preheat the oven to 400°F. Heat the oil in a large frying pan over medium heat. Cook the onion until soft, then add the tomatoes, garlic, bell peppers and celery and cook gently for about 10 minutes. Add the potatoes and oregano and season with salt and pepper, stirring everything together. Tip the mixture onto a baking sheet and cook in the oven for about 30 minutes.

For the cherry tomatoes: Put the tomatoes on a separate baking sheet and toss with the oil, garlic and parsley. Season with salt and pepper. When the potatoes and bell peppers are halfway cooked, put the cherry tomatoes in the oven to cook for 15 minutes.

Heat a barbecue, a chargrill pan or a frying pan and brush it with oil. Cook the fish for about 2–3 minutes each side, turning gently. Brush the cooked sides with the excess marinade.

To serve, arrange the potatoes and bell peppers in the center of 4 plates. Place a piece of swordfish on top and spoon over the cherry tomatoes.

# Roast baby snapper, trussed tomatoes

Every time I cook this dish I feel even more Mediterranean! Its inspiration comes from many years of dreaming of visiting Sicily. Summer days spent under the *loggia* looking out to sea, the chattering of quiet conversation, drifting off to sleep in someone's arms . . .

Serve this dish with a leafy green salad and toasted ciabatta brushed with lemon juice and olive oil, seasoned with salt and pepper.

Serves 6

1 1/3 pounds trussed cherry tomatoes
2 garlic cloves, finely sliced
2 small red chilies, finely sliced
1 cup black olives
14-ounce can diced Italian tomatoes
handful of basil leaves

handful of parsley
1/3 cup red wine vinegar
1 cup olive oil, plus a little extra
salt and freshly ground black pepper
six 7–11-ounce baby snapper,
    scaled and cleaned

Preheat the oven to 350°F. Cut each truss of tomatoes through the stems so that you end up with 6 smaller clusters of tomatoes. Place them in a large baking dish with the garlic, chilies, olives, tomatoes, basil, parsley, vinegar and 1 cup olive oil. Season with salt and pepper. Roast in the oven for about 15 minutes.

Meanwhile, cut the fins from the snapper, and make a cut on both sides of each fish at the thickest part to enable the flavors to penetrate. Season the fish well and brush with the extra oil.

Take the tomato dish out of the oven and scrape the ingredients to the sides. Lay the snapper in the dish and spoon the tomatoes and pan juices back over the top of the fish. Roast for 30 minutes, or until the fish are just cooked.

# Pumpkin, ricotta and herb pizza

There has to be at least one pizza recipe in this book and this one always gets eaten as soon as it is cooked. There is something comforting about pumpkin. Even the word said slowly—p-u-m-p-k-i-n—has a lovely sound. There's nothing more satisfying than enjoying a pizza which you have made from scratch yourself, especially when it's topped with crumbled fresh ricotta, rosemary and thyme.

Makes 2 large pizzas

DOUGH
2¼ cups lukewarm water
two ¼-ounce packets instant dry yeast
¼ teaspoon sugar
1 teaspoon salt
4 cups all-purpose flour
1 tablespoon olive oil, plus extra for
   brushing

2 pounds pumpkin, peeled and cut
   into chunks
⅓ cup olive oil

4 garlic cloves, crushed
4 rosemary sprigs, leaves picked and chopped
salt and freshly ground black pepper
4 cups grated mozzarella
1¾ cups ricotta
¼ cup grated grana padano
2 long red chilies, thinly sliced diagonally
4 thyme sprigs, leaves picked
grated zest of 1 lemon
extra-virgin olive oil (optional)

For the dough: combine the water, yeast, sugar and salt in a mixing bowl and stir until dissolved. Add the flour and 1 tablespoon oil and mix with your hands until just combined. Transfer the dough to a floured work surface and start kneading. Continue until it feels firm and elastic, which should take about 10 minutes (relax and enjoy it!).

Place the dough in a lightly greased bowl. Brush the top and sides of the dough with the extra oil, then cover with a tea towel and put in a warm spot for about 1 hour or until doubled in size.

Divide the dough into two balls and place in separate lightly greased bowls, brushing with oil as before. Cover and wait until they double in size again.

Meanwhile, preheat the oven to 350°F. Put the pumpkin on a baking sheet and toss with the olive oil, garlic and rosemary. Season with salt and pepper, then roast until tender and golden. Set aside to cool slightly, but keep the oven running.

On a floured surface, flatten a ball of dough and roll it out to your desired shape. You may want to make long, narrow pizzas or more traditional round ones. Place on an oiled baking sheet and repeat with the other ball of dough.

Turn the oven up to 400°F. Brush the pizza bases with oil and season with pepper. Spread with mozzarella, then add the pumpkin and dollops of ricotta. Scatter with grana padano. Bake in the oven for about 20 minutes or until the bases are crisp and the edges are golden brown.

Serve scattered with the chili, thyme and lemon zest and drizzled with a little extra-virgin olive oil, if you wish.

# Poussin ragù, apple, radicchio and celery salad

This is my take on chicken stew as, unlike a true ragù, the tender meat stays on the bone and it is served with potatoes instead of pasta. My father's mother taught my mum how to make this dish. When Mum and Dad were married they lived with my father's family, and it was there that Mum learned how to cook.

Serves 6

6 poussin (baby chickens)
½ cup olive oil
1 onion, finely chopped
1 carrot, finely chopped
1 celery stick, stalk finely chopped, leaves
   finely sliced for salad
6 thyme sprigs
3 garlic cloves, finely chopped
½ teaspoon dried chili flakes
1 cup red wine
5½ pounds ripe tomatoes, skinned, seeded
   and roughly chopped, or six 14-ounce cans
   diced Italian tomatoes
2 pounds red potatoes, peeled and quartered
salt and freshly ground black pepper

SALAD
1 apple, halved, cored and thinly sliced
1 radicchio, leaves torn
1 celery stick, finely sliced (including leaves)
2 tablespoons extra-virgin olive oil
juice of ½ orange
salt and freshly ground black pepper

Work on one chicken at a time and cut off the neck and wing tips, discarding both. With the breasts facing up, split the bird down the middle with a sharp knife. Repeat with the other chickens. Rinse the halves and pat dry.

Heat the oil in a large heavy-based pot. Add the chicken halves and brown them all over (you may need to do this in a few batches depending on the size of your pot). Return the browned chicken halves to the pot and add the onion, carrot, celery and thyme, stirring everything gently. Cook for about 5 minutes, until the onion is soft. Add the garlic and chili flakes and cook over a low heat for another 2 minutes. Add the wine and cook another 5 minutes. Add the tomatoes, cover the pot, and slowly bring to the boil. Cook gently for about 45 minutes, stirring every now and then. You may need to add some water if it seems too dry. Add the potatoes and cook for another 15–20 minutes, or until tender. Season with salt and pepper.

For the salad: combine the ingredients including the extra celery leaves in a bowl and toss. Serve the ragù with the salad on the side.

# Grilled pepper steak, creamy vincotto mushrooms

This is the richest recipe in this book, with the earthiness of the mushrooms, the sweetness of the vincotto and the hot hit of the peppercorns combining beautifully with the steak.

Serves 4

four 1-pound porterhouse steaks
1 tablespoon black peppercorns
1 tablespoon green peppercorns
1 tablespoon pink peppercorns
1 teaspoon coriander seeds
1 teaspoon cumin seeds
salt
2 garlic cloves, peeled
1 small red chili, finely chopped
4 parsley sprigs, leaves picked
4 coriander sprigs, leaves picked
½ cup olive oil, plus extra for frying

MUSHROOMS
⅓ cup olive oil
4 tablespoons butter
1 pound mixed mushrooms such as cremini, shiitake and enoki, trimmed
1 leek (white part only), cut into ⅛-inch slices
2 garlic cloves, crushed
2 tablespoons balsamic vinegar
1 cup chicken stock
2 cups cream
grated zest of 1 small lemon
salt and freshly ground black pepper

4 thyme sprigs, leaves picked
lemon wedges

Lightly pound the steaks with a mallet or rolling pin.

Using a large mortar and pestle, pound the peppercorns, coriander and cumin seeds with a little salt. Pound in the garlic, then add the chili, herbs and oil. Tip the mixture onto a plate and press both sides of the steaks into it to coat well. Marinate the steaks in the refrigerator for about 2 hours then take them out and leave for another hour.

For the mushrooms: heat the oil and butter in a large heavy-based saucepan and add the mushrooms (except the enoki, if using). Don't stir them constantly; let them brown a little, then shake the pan or stir gently and leave them alone again for a while. This way they end up with a crunchier texture. When nicely browned, add the leek and garlic and cook until the leek is soft (about 5 minutes). Add the vincotto and chicken stock and cook on medium heat for about 15 minutes or until the liquid has reduced by half. Add the cream, stirring well. When the liquid comes to the boil again, remove from the heat and add the lemon zest and enoki mushrooms (if using). Season with salt and pepper and keep warm.

Preheat the oven to 400°F. Heat the grill of a barbecue, a chargrill pan or a regular frying pan to medium–high heat and brush it with oil. Cook the steaks for about 5 minutes each side, brushing each cooked side with the excess marinade. Transfer the steaks to a baking sheet (or if you have used a pan and it is ovenproof, leave them in the pan) and roast for about 5 minutes for medium–rare, or until cooked to your liking. Remove the steaks from the oven, cover with foil and leave to rest in a warm place for 15 minutes.

Place the steaks on warm plates and spoon over the mushrooms and sauce. Sprinkle with thyme leaves and serve lemon wedges on the side.

# Roast tomato and mussel soup, almond pesto

When Nonna's fishmonger was unable to supply her with the fish she wanted for her *brodu di pisci* (fish soup; page 130), she'd use a combination of garlic, parsley, chilies and salt pounded to a paste and fried, then use this as a base for the stock. It does taste a little of the sea, strange as that may sound. Her stock is the inspiration for this mussel soup, which I love to cook in summer. Nonna also loved almonds and used them regularly in her cooking, as in this pesto.

Serves 4

ALMOND PESTO
1 cup almonds, toasted
1 garlic clove, chopped
2 large handfuls of basil leaves
2 large handfuls of baby spinach leaves
zest and juice of 1 lemon
salt and freshly ground black pepper
½ cup olive oil

SOUP
4½ pounds ripe tomatoes
1 medium onion, finely chopped

3 garlic cloves: 2 unpeeled, 1 peeled and
   chopped
1 bunch dill, leaves and stems/roots separated
½ cup olive oil
salt and freshly ground black pepper
4 parsley sprigs, chopped
3 small red chilies, chopped
1¼ quarts water
1 pound mussels in the shell
1 medium zucchini, grated

For the almond pesto: put the almonds, garlic, basil, spinach, lemon zest and juice in a food processor and season with salt and pepper. Turn the machine on and begin adding the oil. You need enough to bind the mixture without letting it get too thin, so you may not need to use all of it.

For the soup: preheat the oven to 350°F. Put the tomatoes into a baking dish, gently crushing each one with your hand as you do so. Add the onion, 2 unpeeled garlic cloves, dill roots and stems, and ⅓ cup of the oil, then season with salt and pepper. Mix the ingredients together with your hands, then roast uncovered for about 1 hour, or until the tomatoes break down and are black in places and everything bubbles away in a pool of juice.

Pass everything through a food mill into a clean container or saucepan. This will remove the tomato and garlic skins and dill stalks and roots.

Pound the chopped garlic, parsley, chilies and a little salt to a paste using a mortar and pestle. Heat the remaining oil in a pot. Add the paste and fry over low heat for about 2 minutes. Add the water and bring to the boil, then simmer for 20 minutes.

Meanwhile, scrub the mussel shells with a stiff brush in cold water and pull away the beards. Chop the dill leaves.

Add the tomato mixture and the zucchini to the pot and bring to the boil. Season with salt and pepper. Add the mussels and cover the pot with a lid. Cook until the mussels open, then scoop them onto a plate (discard any that haven't opened). Put the chopped dill in the soup.

Remove the mussels from their shells and divide among warm serving bowls. Ladle the soup over them and top with almond pesto.

# Herb-stuffed baked salmon for Johanne

This is a stuffed side of salmon rather than a whole stuffed fish, and it is lovely served with a peppery watercress and potato salad. I made it for my wife, Johanne, on Mother's Day and she loved it so much she wanted it again for her birthday two weeks later.

Serves 8

2 thick slices sourdough, torn into chunks
½ cup pine nuts
1 garlic clove, chopped
handful of herbs such as parsley, oregano and
    thyme leaves, chopped
pinch of dried chili flakes

one 3–4-pound side salmon, skin on, pin
    bones removed with tweezers
⅓ cup olive oil
salt and freshly ground black pepper
1 bunch dill
2 large lemons, thinly sliced

Preheat the oven to 350°F. Combine the bread, pine nuts, garlic, herbs and chili flakes in a food processor and blend to rough breadcrumbs.

Wash the salmon and pat it dry. Trim off the thin ends and sides to get a rectangle shape (use the off-cuts in another dish, such as pasta) and rub the skin and flesh all over with the oil and salt and pepper. Cut the salmon in half, creating two square-ish pieces.

Lay 4 lengths of string vertically along a work surface, spacing them about 2 inches apart. Place half the stalks of dill in a line over the string and lay one piece of salmon on top, skin-side down. Place a quarter of the lemon slices down the center of the salmon. Press the stuffing onto the salmon, then add another line of lemon. Lay the other salmon half on top, skin-side up, matching the thick end of the bottom piece to the thin end of the top piece so you get a roughly even thickness all over.

Cover the salmon with the remaining dill stalks and tie up the pieces of string, securing the fish pieces together. Don't tie too tightly, just enough to secure everything in place.

Lay the rest of the lemon slices on the base of a tray and place the stuffed salmon on top. Bake in the oven for 30–35 minutes. The thicker parts should still be a little rare in the middle, although, if you don't like it this way, cook for a little longer. Let the salmon rest for 5 minutes, then transfer it to a serving platter and cut the string. Slice the salmon with a sharp knife—it will fall apart as you do so. Make sure you provide stuffing and lemon with each serving.

# Roast chicken breast, herbed goat's cheese stuffing, arugula sauce

Many people love to serve stuffed chicken breasts fanned out on a plate, but try cutting into wider chunks and serving them on a large platter drizzled with this lovely nutty, peppery arugula sauce.

Serves 4

STUFFING
7 ounces fresh goat's cheese
½ cup grated pepper pecorino
¼ cup fresh breadcrumbs
1 garlic clove, finely chopped
3 parsley sprigs, finely chopped
2 rosemary sprigs, leaves finely chopped
3 thyme sprigs, leaves picked
8 chives, finely chopped
zest and juice of 1 small lemon
2 anchovies, chopped

4 free-range chicken breasts, skin on
⅓ cup olive oil
4 tablespoons butter
4 rosemary sprigs, leaves picked
2 garlic cloves, sliced

ARUGULA SAUCE
3 handfuls of arugula, chopped
2 handfuls of spinach leaves, chopped
½ cup macadamias, roasted
1 garlic clove, chopped
½ cup olive oil
½ cup cream
salt and freshly ground black pepper

For the stuffing: combine the ingredients in a bowl and mix thoroughly. Oil a baking sheet.

Take the first chicken breast and gently insert your fingers under the skin, easing the skin away from the flesh, to create a large pocket for the stuffing. Spoon the stuffing under the skin, gently pushing it as far as it will go. Stretch the skin over the stuffing and tuck it under the breast, and place the breast on the baking sheet. Repeat with the other chicken breasts.

Preheat the oven to 400°F. Drizzle the chicken breasts with the olive oil and dot with the butter. Spread the rosemary and garlic slices all over and roast for 40–45 minutes, or until the chicken is golden brown.

For the arugula sauce: combine the arugula, spinach, macadamias and garlic in a food processor and blend until finely chopped. Add the oil and cream and process until smooth. Transfer to a bowl and season with salt and pepper.

To serve, either cut the chicken breasts into thick slices so the stuffing shows or leave them whole. Place on plates and drizzle with the arugula sauce.

# Chargrilled sardines, walnut gremolata, green bean and beet salad, pesto mayonnaise

Sweet, smoky sardines with a scattering of nutty garlic breadcrumbs make the perfect lunch, full of flavor and with a seductive array of textures and colors. The inspiration for this dish is classic Sicilian stuffed sardines, but here they're served with a good dollop of pesto mayonnaise.

Serves 4

PESTO MAYONNAISE
1 tablespoon pesto
⅓ cup mayonnaise
2 tablespoons mascarpone
4 dill sprigs, finely chopped

GREEN BEAN AND BEET SALAD
7 ounces green beans, topped and tailed
4 ounces snow peas, topped, tailed and strung
1 beet, peeled and grated
2 handfuls of baby spinach leaves
½ bunch mint, leaves picked
1 spring onion, thinly sliced diagonally
1 cup shaved grana padano
1 tablespoon extra-virgin olive oil
salt and freshly ground black pepper

WALNUT GREMOLATA
¼ cup olive oil
1 garlic clove, finely chopped
½ cup walnuts, finely chopped
½ cup currants
1 cup fresh breadcrumbs
2 tablespoons finely chopped parsley
2 tablespoons finely sliced mint leaves
salt and freshly ground black pepper

16 fresh sardine fillets, washed
  and patted dry
salt and freshly ground black pepper
lemon wedges

For the mayonnaise: combine the ingredients and set aside.

For the salad: bring a large saucepan of salted water to the boil. Put the beans in the water, bring back to the boil and cook for about 3 minutes. Add the snow peas, then quickly drain the beans and peas and tip them into a large bowl of ice water. Drain again when thoroughly cool. Cut the snow peas into thin strips lengthwise. Combine beans and peas in a bowl with the beet, spinach, mint, spring onion, grana padano and oil. Season with salt and pepper, lightly toss and set aside.

For the gremolata: heat the oil in a frying pan over low heat. Add the garlic and fry for 30 seconds without browning. Add the remaining ingredients and cook for about 5 minutes or until the breadcrumbs are light golden. Season with salt and pepper and remove from the heat.

Heat a barbecue, a chargrill pan or a regular frying pan and brush it with oil. Season the sardine fillets with salt and pepper. Place half the fillets on the grill skin-side down. By the time you have placed the last fillet, the first one should be ready to turn. The fillets should cook for about 1 minute each side. Transfer the cooked fillets, skin-side down, to a baking sheet to keep warm while you continue cooking the other half.

Toss the salad once more and spoon onto 4 plates. Lay 4 sardine fillets on top of each salad and scatter the warm gremolata around the fish. Top with a spoonful of pesto mayonnaise and serve with lemon wedges.

# Rhubarb and ricotta tart, honey and cinnamon yogurt

The sour cream pastry recipe here is Maggie Beer's. It's a foolproof pastry, the one that works for me every time, and so versatile that it can be used for both sweet and savory tarts. It works just as well with yogurt instead of sour cream, and makes a terrific, rustic-looking crostata. You can leave it overnight to chill, but in colder months I use it straightaway. It never separates and you can be as rough as you like with it.

Serves 12

SOUR CREAM PASTRY
1 cup chilled butter, chopped
2 cups all-purpose flour
½ cup sour cream

1 egg, beaten

FILLING
10 rhubarb stalks, cut diagonally into
    1-inch lengths
⅔ cup sugar
2 tablespoons brandy
½ cup water

TOPPING
⅓ pound ricotta
½ pound mascarpone
½ cup superfine sugar
grated zest of 1 lime
2 eggs

HONEY AND CINNAMON YOGURT
1 cup natural yogurt
1 tablespoon honey
pinch of cinnamon

To make the pastry: pulse the butter and flour in a food processor until the mixture resembles breadcrumbs. Add the sour cream and pulse until the dough just forms a ball. Wrap the dough in plastic wrap and refrigerate for 20 minutes.

Brush a 10-inch tart pan with a removable base with melted butter and dust it with flour, shaking out the excess. Roll the dough out on a floured work surface and line the pan with it, trimming any excess pastry. Refrigerate for another 30 minutes (or freeze at this stage if you are making the pastry in advance).

For the filling: put the rhubarb in a saucepan with the sugar, brandy and water and cook over low heat for 15–20 minutes, until tender. Don't stir it too much, as you want the rhubarb to keep some shape. Set aside to cool.

For the topping: combine the topping ingredients in a bowl and stir until smooth.

For the yogurt: combine the ingredients and set aside.

Preheat the oven to 350°F. Cover the chilled pastry shell with parchment paper and fill it with baking weights, rice or beans. Bake for 10 minutes, then remove the paper and weights and bake for another 5 minutes or until cooked. Brush the shell with the beaten egg and bake for a final 5 minutes, or until light brown.

Lower the oven temperature to 325°F. Spread the cooled rhubarb over the baked tart shell. Cover with the ricotta mixture and bake in the oven for about 20 minutes or until the topping has set. Let the tart cool a little before removing from the pan and slicing and serving with the yogurt.

Extravagance
Generosity
/ Love
Tradition
Life
Food

To Papa

I love you, Dad.

Pauloino

X X X X X X
X X X X X X

All the pasta recipes in this book have
been collected here in this chapter. I love
pasta. I could eat it every day for lunch,
in any way, shape or style, and I'd be
happy. Happy for me does not come easy,
it's hard work, but give me a plate
of spaccatelle with broad beans and my
heart is smiling, as is my stomach, my eyes,
my head and my mouth. And every time
I see Mrs Mirabella (the one this book is
dedicated to), my body and mind react
the same. I love going to Paris with her,
watching her being seduced by this
most enchanting city. Walking, talking
and soaking up the sun in Jardin du
Luxembourg – eating long thin crunchy
baguettes and drinking beer. Going only
halfway up the Eiffel Tower with her
and then catching a ferry along
the Seine at night and falling in love
with our Paris under the stars.
Being overwhelmed, tired, hot, fighting
and lost in Barcelona. But then
discovering tapas for the first time
together and the Cuines Santa
Caterina Restaurant, eating lunch
and dinner there every day. Love
can be tough, but it can also be the easiest
thing in the world to do.

—
About a year ago, as I was
leaving the house to go to
work early one morning, I
noticed a bulging black
plastic bag beside the
front door.
—

My wife Johanne called to me from the kitchen, reminding me to take the bag to the thrift shop, if I wouldn't mind.

Curious to see what was inside, I untied the knot. My heart skipped a beat as I drew out a handful of sheer, midnight-blue fabric. It was the first dress I ever bought for Johanne. I got it at the Bell Book and Candle boutique in South Yarra, in 1973. I pressed the fabric to my face, closed my eyes and saw us both as teenagers. The silhouette of Johanne's body in front of me, the way the skirt moved from side to side as she walked. I sighed deeply and smiled, and every one of the thirty-five years since that moment flashed by.

I reached into the bag once again and untangled a pale green frock with a slippery beige silk lining. The label read Garb Shop, Block Arcade, Collins Street, Melbourne. Jo looked gorgeous in this dress, though now it was definitely retro chic.

I took out many other dresses from that black plastic bag. A very feminine, off-the-shoulder black velvet Laura Ashley evening gown. A Gatsby-style beige dress with a matching jacket, that Johanne had worn to my twenty-first birthday party and that belonged in the bag. A black taffeta dress from the '80s that definitely belonged in the bag.

Johanne's sense of style is original and personal. One of her favorite garments is my no-nonsense Roy Rogers red parka, given to me by my Italian cousin Paolo. It's the thing she loves to wear when she goes to the soccer stadium, its pale yellow plastic hood keeping her warm and dry while she is watching her beloved team. In a sea of black and white, there she is in bright red, intensely watching the game.

Every year, on the Queen's birthday weekend, Jo,
Pam and Paul, who all barrack for Collingwood, and
Danielle and I, who love to watch Melbourne beat them,
go to the game. I usually bring along a newspaper and
magazines to read, and only really start to get into
it by the third quarter, especially if my team is in
front. And there's Jo scrutinizing every kick from
the very first bounce of the ball. Sometimes sulking,
reprimanding or praising players; at other times
jumping for joy and screaming.

I watch my wife and think "who is this person?"
After all these years spent watching, I'm still
trying to work her out. And that's what I love.

We fight, we talk and we walk. We laugh and laugh,
and thank God we still play. I am learning to listen,
and listen better. I don't like soccer as much as
Jo and she doesn't like cooking, but I love eating her
food and cherish our conversations at the end of the
day, and watching movies on Sunday afternoons.

—

Caro D~

Sono co~
~malatt~
mio pi~
Amor mi~
ci parler~
parlarem~
ditino

mirabella '00

mirabella '00

JOHN FITZGERALD KENNEDY
A Life in Pictures

Calder

Brennan & Brennan    Goat Cheese    CHRONICLE BOOKS

FRENCH DREAMS    Steven Rothfeld    HOPMANN

A CONSIDERABLE TOWN    M.F.K. FISHER    KNOPF

The Nature of Gardens    Peter Timms

THE COMPLETE OSCAR WILDE    Stories, Plays and Poems    TIGER

1421    The Year China Discovered America    GAVIN MENZIES

ITALIAN STYLE    Jane Gordon-Clark

SPICES

PETER ROBB    MIDNIGHT IN SICILY

David Gilmour    THE LAST LEOPARD

DRAWN FROM LIFE    JOHN OLSEN    HEADLINE

ANTONY WORRALL THOMPSON    Modern Bistrot Cookery    HEADLINE

Picasso

Picasso

VEUREMIRÓ    La irradiació de Miró en l'art espanyol    Fundació "la Caixa"

Walking the Dog in Italy    VIKING

Raf Artugal    Scholte    KÖNEMANN

Love takes you home    JULIE CAPALDO

ITALIAN PLEASURES    HARVEY & MITCHELL

THERESA MAGGIO    The STONE BOUDOIR

The Leopard    Giuseppe Tomasi di Lampedusa

the IMPRESSIONIST    hari kunzru

THE JOSEPH BROWN COLLECTION AT NGV AUSTRALIA

Picasso Twentieth Century 1901-1972

Collection    Museo Picasso Málaga

love &

love

love (

love &

love

love &

love (

love (

love &

love

# Rigatoni, tomatoes, baby prawns, salmon

Pasta with seafood is one of my favorites. Simple, as it is here, with lots of fresh herbs over the top. I really don't want to share this recipe with anyone, but then that's not really the spirit of "love," is it?

Serves 4

½ cup olive oil

1 medium onion, finely chopped

1 small carrot, finely chopped

1 celery stick, finely chopped

2 garlic cloves, finely sliced

¼ teaspoon dried chili flakes

4 dill sprigs, chopped, plus extra leaves
   to serve

4 parsley stalks, chopped, plus extra leaves
   to serve

3 pounds ripe tomatoes, coarsely chopped,
   or three 14-ounce cans diced Italian
   tomatoes

handful of basil leaves

1 teaspoon sugar

salt and freshly ground black pepper

1 pound rigatoni

1 pound salmon fillets, skinned, pin bones
   removed with tweezers, cut into chunks

7 ounces shelled small raw prawns (without
   heads or tails)

zest and juice of 1 lemon

grana padano (optional)

Heat ⅓ cup of the oil in a large saucepan and gently fry the onion, carrot and celery until the onion is translucent. Add the garlic, chili flakes, dill and parsley and cook for another 3 minutes. Add the tomatoes, cover the pan and slowly bring to the boil. Simmer over a low heat for about 30 minutes, partially covered. Add the basil and sugar and season with salt and pepper. Keep warm.

Cook the pasta in a pot of salted boiling water until al dente.

Meanwhile, season the salmon and prawns with salt and pepper. Heat the remaining oil in a frying pan and cook the seafood for about 4 minutes, stirring occasionally. Turn off the heat when the prawns are cooked; the fish should still be slightly underdone, as it will cook a little more in the sauce.

Drain the pasta and return it to the pot. Add the lemon zest and juice, a little of the sauce and all of the seafood and toss. Serve on individual plates with more of the sauce spooned on top. Scatter with the extra dill and parsley leaves. Italians don't like cheese with their seafood but I can't resist a little grana padano on my pasta, so add if desired.

# Pasta di verdura

This dish fits somewhere between a soup and a pasta, and is usually made with whatever vegetables (*verdura*) are growing in the garden. My family has always believed that a big bowl of pasta di verdura will cure, or at least soothe, any cold or flu. Almost everything goes in at once, so it's easy as well as good for you.

Serves 4–6

salt and freshly ground black pepper

1 pound linguine, broken into 1-inch lengths

2–3 celery sticks, finely chopped

1 carrot, finely chopped

4 red potatoes, peeled and
   cut into ⅓-inch cubes

1 small zucca lunga (about 8 inches long) or
   2 medium zuccchinis, cut into ⅓-inch cubes

7 ounces green beans, topped and tailed,
   sliced diagonally into ⅓-inch pieces

2–3 Swiss chard stalks, leaves finely sliced,
   stalks chopped

7 ounces young fava beans, shelled (to
   make about 4 ounces beans)

1 cup shelled peas, fresh or frozen

2 parsley sprigs, finely chopped

2 basil sprigs, finely chopped

2 dill sprigs, finely chopped

2 handfuls of arugula

2 handfuls of baby spinach leaves

2 tablespoons extra-virgin olive oil,
   plus more to serve

4–6 poached eggs (optional)

grated grana padano

Bring 2 quarts of water to the boil in a large pot. Season with salt and pepper and add all the ingredients except for the herbs, arugula, spinach and oil. Cook until the pasta is al dente and the vegetables are tender. Take off the heat and add the remaining ingredients and stir. Check the seasoning.

   To serve, ladle the soup into bowls and add a poached egg, if desired. Drizzle with more oil and serve grated grana padano at the table for guests to help themselves.

# Linguine, broccoli, basil, cherry tomatoes

This recipe is perfect for an easy, healthful, Mediterranean-style pasta if you don't have much time, as only the pasta and broccoli need to be cooked. The inspiration comes from growing up on a farm, at a time when broccoli was the only vegetable Dad grew. Creativity is paramount when you are limited to a single green vegetable! The ricotta is either dolloped, if you use the softer variety, or crumbled, if you like your ricotta firm. Either way, quickly grab a fork and get into it.

Serves 4

1 pound broccoli, cut into small florets
salt
1 pound linguine
handful of basil leaves
2 garlic cloves, crushed
½ cup olive oil

freshly ground black pepper
7 ounces baby spinach leaves
7 ounces cherry tomatoes, halved
1 cup grated grana padano ·
½ pound ricotta

Cook the broccoli in a pot of salted boiling water until just tender. Remove with a slotted spoon and set aside to drain. Cook the pasta in the same water until al dente.

Meanwhile, combine the broccoli, basil, garlic and olive oil in a bowl and season with salt and pepper.

Drain the pasta, reserving 1 cup of the cooking water, and return both to the pot. Add the broccoli mixture, spinach, tomatoes and grana padano and toss well. Serve topped with the ricotta.

# Spaccatelle, fava beans

I'm especially fond of fava beans; they remind me of the time my father planted a crop of them before he went away one winter, and left my younger brother, Frank, in charge of caring for them. Dad timed his absence perfectly, for when he returned, the beans were ready to pick.

The fava bean sauce goes perfectly with the spaccatelle pasta. It's a short, curved, tube-like pasta that holds the sauce like a spoon. A variation of this pasta is to add salted dry ricotta (*ricotta salata*), which is available from good Italian delis, or fresh ricotta, and mix it through at the end.

Serves 4

6 pounds fava beans in their pods
½ cup olive oil
1 small onion, finely chopped
1 leek (white part only), finely chopped
1 small carrot, finely chopped
1 celery stick, finely chopped
1 quart boiling water
salt and freshly ground black pepper
1 pound spaccatelle or other short pasta
4 dill sprigs, leaves picked

Shell the fava beans, then peel the individual beans by cutting one end with a knife and peeling off the skins with your fingers. This is a good job to share with someone.

Heat the oil in heavy-based saucepan. Add the onion, leek, carrot and celery and fry gently until the onion is translucent. Add the fava beans and cook for another 15 minutes, stirring occasionally. Add the boiling water and season with salt and pepper. Cook for about 45 minutes, partially covered. Mash the beans with a fork from time to time. By the end the sauce should be a chunky purée.

Cook the pasta in a pot of salted boiling water until al dente. Drain and return to the pot. Stir through the fava bean sauce and dill and serve.

# Potato gnocchi, roast tomato Napoli

A few years ago we had a bright young chef named Robbie Wright working at the café; I'm sure he won't mind me using his recipe for gnocchi and tomato sauce here. Not only is it easy to prepare, the lovely sweet flavors of tomatoes, garlic and herbs, combined with a kick of balsamic, are rustic and gorgeous. Of course, there are many other sauces you could serve with gnocchi, including burnt butter and sage, almond pesto (page 57), pea (page 90) or fava bean (page 77).

Serves 6

NAPOLI SAUCE
4½ pounds ripe tomatoes
1 garlic head
large handful of herbs such as oregano,
    thyme and basil leaves
1 rosemary sprig, leaves picked
¼ cup olive oil
⅓ cup balsamic vinegar
salt and freshly ground black pepper

GNOCCHI
3 pounds waxy potatoes, peeled
1 tablespoon salt
few gratings of fresh nutmeg
2 eggs
3 cups all-purpose flour

grana padano

To make the Napoli sauce: preheat the oven to 350°F. Squish the tomatoes with your hands to open them up, and put them in a deep roasting dish. Break up the head of garlic without peeling the cloves and add to the tomatoes. Add the herbs, oil and vinegar and season with salt and pepper.

Roast in the oven uncovered for about 1 hour, or until the tomatoes break down and are black in places and everything bubbles away in a pool of juice.

Pass everything through a food mill into a saucepan. This will remove the tomato and garlic skins. Season with salt and pepper and set aside.

To make the gnocchi: cook the potatoes in a large pot of boiling water until tender but not falling apart. Drain and allow them to dry for a few minutes. Pass them through a food mill or potato ricer into a large bowl (if you don't have either of these, use a masher and mash as smooth as possible). Mix in the salt, nutmeg and eggs. Add the flour and loosely press it into the potatoes with your fingers until the mixture begins to come together as dough. It should spring back when lightly pressed. If it seems too sticky you may need a little extra flour. Don't knead or overwork the dough or the gnocchi will end up gluey and tough.

Put the dough on a floured work surface. Roll it into thin sausages and cut them diagonally into ¾-inch pieces. Cook batches of gnocchi in salted boiling water until they tumble freely on the surface. Remove from the water with a slotted spoon and drain.

To serve, heat the sauce and stir some through the cooked gnocchi. Pile onto serving plates and spoon more Napoli over the top if you wish. Pass around the grana padano.

If you want to prepare gnocchi in advance, plunge the cooked gnocchi into iced water to cool, then drain and toss in a little olive oil. Store in an airtight container in the refrigerator for 2–3 days, or even freeze. Gently reheat the gnocchi and Napoli together in a saucepan.

# Roast pumpkin and asparagus lasagne

Pumpkin and asparagus make a terrific double act. The sweet taste and soft texture of pumpkin plays beautifully with the crispness and unique flavor of asparagus. I know I'm not supposed to use cream with pasta so if you're feeling a little guilty, as I sometimes do, you can omit the cream and just use ricotta or mascarpone or both. Or, why not forget the guilt and serve small portions of the lasagne prepared with just a little ricotta, grana padano and cream for this rich and deliciously decadent dish.

Serves 8–10

2 pounds pumpkin, peeled and cut
   into ¾-inch cubes
½ cup olive oil
4 garlic cloves, halved
1 onion, finely chopped
½ bunch sage, leaves picked
½ bunch thyme, leaves picked
few gratings of fresh nutmeg

salt and freshly ground black pepper
½ bunch chives, chopped
1 pound ricotta
10 dried lasagne sheets
1½ cups cream
12 asparagus spears, ends trimmed,
   sliced into 1-inch pieces
2 cups grated grana padano

Preheat the oven to 350°F. Put the pumpkin pieces on a baking sheet and toss with the oil, garlic, onion, half the sage and thyme, and the nutmeg. Season with salt and pepper, then roast in the oven until tender and golden. Remove from the oven and allow to cool a little (but keep the oven on). Discard the garlic and put the mixture in a bowl. Add the chives and ricotta and mash everything together.

Meanwhile, cook the lasagne sheets in a large pot of salted boiling water until just al dente. Drain and cool under running water. Lightly brush the sheets with oil on both sides so they don't stick together and lay them on a plate.

Oil or butter a baking dish and pour a little of the cream into the base. Place 2 lasagne sheets over the cream. Spread some of the pumpkin mixture over the top and scatter with some asparagus, then with some of the remaining sage and thyme, then with grana padano. Add more cream and lasagne sheets and continue layering. Top with the final pieces of lasagne, the remaining pumpkin, asparagus, cream and grana padano. Scatter with the remaining thyme and press the last sage leaves over the surface. Bake for 30–40 minutes, or until golden. Rest for 15 minutes before serving.

# Cauliflower, ricotta and herb ravioli

There is nothing more pleasurable than making your own ravioli and it's even more fun if there are two of you, especially when it comes to rolling the pasta through the pasta machine. Make sure you have good ingredients, the right utensils, plenty of bench space, more than enough time, some music playing in the background, a bottle of red wine, sunshine in your heart and a smile on your face. This is the love chapter, after all!

Serves 6

SAUCE
¼ cup olive oil
1 onion, chopped
1 carrot, chopped
1 celery stick, chopped
pinch of dried chili flakes
2–3 sprigs oregano, leaves picked
1 garlic clove, chopped
4 pounds ripe tomatoes, skinned, seeded
   and roughly chopped, or four 14-ounce
   cans diced Italian tomatoes
½ cup butter
1 teaspoon sugar
salt and freshly ground black pepper

FILLING
1 medium cauliflower, cut into florets
salt
3 garlic cloves, crushed
pinch of dried chili flakes
1 cup grated grana padano
⅔ pound ricotta

⅓ pound fresh goat's cheese
handful of herbs such as parsley, basil,
   thyme and sage leaves, chopped
2 anchovies, chopped
freshly ground black pepper

PASTA
3¼ cups all-purpose flour
pinch of salt
1 teaspoon olive oil
4 eggs, plus 1 extra egg lightly beaten

grana padano or pecorino

For the sauce: heat the oil in a large saucepan and gently fry the onion, carrot, celery, chili flakes and oregano until the onion is translucent. Add the garlic and cook for 30 seconds without browning. Add the tomatoes and bring to a simmer, cooking for 45–60 minutes. Stir in the butter and sugar and season with salt and pepper. Give the sauce a whiz with a hand-held blender.

For the filling: cook the cauliflower in a pot of salted boiling water until tender. Drain and leave to cool. Put the cauliflower and remaining ingredients in a food processor and blend until just combined. Don't let it purée, as you want some chunkiness.

For the pasta: clean out the food processor and add the flour, salt and oil. Turn the motor on and begin adding the 4 eggs, one at a time, until the dough just comes together. Remove the dough from the food processor and knead on a lightly floured surface for 5 minutes. Cover the dough in plastic wrap and refrigerate for 30 minutes.

Cut the dough into four even pieces and cover three with a cloth. Roll the first piece through a pasta machine at its widest setting. Fold the piece in half and put it through again—do this about 10 times, until the pasta is smooth. Now roll the pasta through on increasingly narrow settings until you reach 1½ notches from the narrowest. Place the sheet on a floured surface and roll out the remaining dough.

Working quickly, lay a pasta sheet lengthwise in front of you and place tablespoon-sized dollops of filling in a row across one half, spacing them about 2 inches apart. There should be room for about 4 or 5 ravioli on each half sheet. Lightly brush the beaten egg around each filling and fold the other half of the pasta sheet over the top, gently laying it across the mounds. Push out any trapped air and press the sheets together around each filling to seal. With a pasta cutter or a knife, cut between the rows of ravioli and place them on a floured surface. Repeat with the remaining pasta sheets and filling, then roll any pasta scraps through the machine to make more ravioli. As the filling is moist, don't leave the ravioli sitting for too long before you cook them. (To prepare in advance, it is best to cook the ravioli straight away and then reheat in a pot of boiling water.)

Cook the ravioli in a large pot of salted boiling water for 8–10 minutes or until they float to the surface. While the ravioli is cooking, reheat the sauce. Drain the ravioli and serve 3 per person with the sauce spooned over the top. Serve grana padano or pecorino at the table.

# Linguine, zucchini, spinach, lemon, pine nuts

This is the most popular pasta we've ever served in the café, and it continues to appear on the menu every day. We may vary it a little by adding roasted pumpkin or potatoes, as it's the most versatile pasta there is. You might like to add cooked, still bright green peas or ripe cherry tomatoes. Or instead of pine nuts, you could try roasted flaked almonds or chopped hazelnuts, which two of our favorite customers, Jan and Bob Bluck, love the best.

Jan and Bob have lunch with us every day at the café, sitting together on the same side of the table with a glass of pinot, talking and laughing. Bob is eighty and Jan is sixty-nine. Bob has little heart-shaped pieces of material on his denim shirts that Jan has sewn on to patch up the tears he gets from working in the garden. Jan wears the most interesting chain necklace that has miniature cars dangling from it. They both adore cars and drive around Mount Eliza in one of those old convertible French Citroën taxis. It in turn has a love heart sewn onto the roof to cover a torn patch where Jan drove into the branch of a tree.

Serves 12

3 pounds linguine
salt
1½ cups pine nuts, toasted
4 medium zucchini, grated
4 large handfuls of baby spinach leaves
zest and juice of 2 large lemons
2 garlic cloves, crushed
½ cup olive oil
freshly ground black pepper

Cook the linguine in a large pot of salted boiling water until al dente.

Drain the pasta and return it to the pot. Add the rest of the ingredients and season with salt and plenty of pepper.

Gently toss everything together and serve.

# Fusilli, tomatoes, basil, garlic

This is probably the quickest and one of the most flavorsome pasta recipes in this chapter. It's another family favorite, especially when people drop in to visit and stay for lunch or dinner. We eat this pasta all the way through summer and into early autumn as the tomatoes slowly start to disappear.

Serves 4

1 pound fusilli
salt
¼ cup olive oil
2 garlic cloves, finely chopped
4 ripe tomatoes, chopped
2 large handfuls of basil leaves, torn, plus
    extra to serve
1 cup grated grana padano,
    plus extra to serve
freshly ground black pepper

Cook the pasta in a pot of salted boiling water until al dente.

Meanwhile, heat the oil in a frying pan and add the garlic, and cook for 30 seconds without browning. Add the tomatoes and cook for about 3 minutes. Add the basil and grana padano and season with salt and pepper.

Drain the pasta, return it to the pot and toss the sauce through it. Divide among plates and scatter with more basil and grana padano.

# Pasta con le sardi

Mum calls this recipe pasta Milanese, which one presumes means it comes from Milan in northern Italy. But I have a hunch it was probably Sicilian and taught to her by one of my grandmothers, who in turn was given the recipe by a friend who was from Milan. In Sicily, where it is a classic dish of the island, they incorporate breadcrumbs, pine nuts and currants for that hit of *agrodolce* (sweet and sour) that they love so much. Whatever the origin, it is a truly satisfying dish.

Serves 6

SAUCE
½ cup olive oil
1 medium onion, finely chopped
⅔ cup wild fennel greens (tender stems only)
   or dill, finely chopped
14 ounces fresh sardines, cleaned and boned,
   heads and tails removed
4½ pounds ripe tomatoes, skinned, seeded
   and coarsely chopped, or four 14-ounce
   cans diced Italian tomatoes
salt and freshly ground pepper

TOPPING
½ cup olive oil
1 cup fresh breadcrumbs
2 garlic cloves, crushed
4 tablespoons finely chopped parsley
½ cup pine nuts
½ cup currants
2 teaspoons sugar

1 pound spaghetti

For the sauce: heat ⅓ cup of the oil in a saucepan and gently fry the onion until translucent. Add the wild fennel and a little more oil and continue to cook, as Mum would say until the aromas start to fill the kitchen. Add the sardines and continue to fry for about 10 minutes, until they begin to break up.

Add the tomatoes and slowly bring to the boil. Cook on a medium heat for about 20 minutes. Season with salt and pepper.

For the topping: heat the oil in a frying pan and add all of the ingredients. Gently fry until the breadcrumbs and pine nuts are lightly toasted or a light golden brown.

Meanwhile, bring water to the boil in a large pot, add salt and cook the pasta until al dente. Drain and return to the pot. Add the sauce, gently toss and serve on individual plates. Serve the breadcrumb and pine nut topping at the table for your guests to help themselves.

# Conchiglioni, artichoke and spinach pesto, goat's cheese

I love the way beautiful, big, bold shell pasta holds the sauce inside its cavity, so you get an explosion of texture and taste with every mouthful.

Serves 6

PESTO
one 14-ounce can artichoke hearts in brine,
    drained
2 garlic cloves, finely chopped
large handful of baby spinach leaves
large handful of basil leaves
1 cup olive oil
freshly ground black pepper

1 pound conchiglioni
salt
1 tablespoon olive oil
1 garlic clove, finely chopped
1 cup fresh breadcrumbs
2 tablespoons finely chopped parsley
freshly ground black pepper
1 cup grated grana padano
½ pound fresh goat's cheese

For the pesto: put the artichokes, garlic, spinach, basil and oil in a food processor and purée. Season with pepper.

Cook the pasta in a pot of salted boiling water until al dente (this pasta takes longer to cook than most others). Meanwhile, heat the oil in a frying pan. Add the garlic and fry gently for 30 seconds without browning. Add the breadcrumbs and parsley and cook until the breadcrumbs are nicely toasted. Season with salt and pepper.

Drain the pasta, reserving half a cup of the cooking water, and return the pasta and water to the pot. Add the grana padano and pesto and stir everything through. Divide among plates, crumbling goat's cheese onto each serve and scattering with the breadcrumb mixture.

# Canneroni, peas, mascarpone, thyme

For as long as I can remember, this pasta dish has been a family favorite. Many years ago, my cousin Frank, who was about seven or eight at the time, came to stay on our farm for the holidays. My mother served this pasta, which little Frank refused to eat. Dad, who was sitting beside him and getting impatient, leaned over, grabbed Frank's plate of pasta and very calmly proceeded to tip it over Frankie's head. My mother, brother Frank and sister Josie were stunned, their mouths open. Darling Josie, who was close to my cousin, quietly started crying. We resumed our dinner in silence while my young cousin sat there covered in a dripping green mess, sobbing. Frank went on to become a successful greengrocer, lovingly displaying his fruit and vegetables, especially his peas.

Serves 4

⅓ cup olive oil
1 small onion, finely chopped
1 celery stick, finely chopped
3 cups shelled peas (fresh or frozen)
1 quart boiling water

salt and freshly ground black pepper
¾ pound canneroni or other short pasta
3½ ounces mascarpone
4 thyme sprigs, leaves picked
extra-virgin olive oil (optional)

Heat the oil in a heavy-based saucepan. Add the onion and celery and gently fry until the onion is translucent. Add the peas and cook over low heat for 15 minutes, stirring occasionally. Add the boiling water and season with salt and pepper. Cook, partially covered, for about 45 minutes. Mash the peas from time to time. By the end the sauce should be a chunky purée.

Cook the pasta in a pot of salted boiling water until al dente. Drain and return the pasta to the pot. Stir in the pea sauce and divide among plates. Top each serving with a dollop of mascarpone and scatter with thyme leaves. Drizzle with some extra-virgin olive oil, if you like.

# Broccoli and spinach lasagne

This stylish lasagne is fantastically green! It's teamed here with ricotta, for a lighter touch, but if you prefer a béchamel or cheese sauce, go right ahead. Whatever you love most!

Serves 8–10

1 pound broccoli, roughly chopped
salt
1 pound baby spinach leaves
10 dried lasagne sheets
olive oil
handful of herbs such as thyme,
    parsley and sage leaves

½ teaspoon freshly grated nutmeg
1 pound ricotta
zest and juice of 1 lemon
2 cups grated grana padano
freshly ground black pepper

Cook the broccoli in a large pot of salted boiling water until tender. Add ¾ pound of the spinach. As soon as it has wilted, remove everything with a slotted spoon and set aside.

Return the water to the boil and add the lasagne sheets, cooking until just al dente. Drain (reserving 1 cup of the cooking water) and cool the lasagne under running water. Lightly brush the sheets with oil on both sides so they don't stick together and lay them on a plate.

Put the broccoli, spinach, reserved cooking water, herbs, nutmeg, ricotta, lemon zest and juice and grana padano in a food processor and season with salt and pepper. Blend until smooth.

Preheat the oven to 350°F. Oil or butter a baking dish. Spread a little of the ricotta mixture in the bottom of the dish and top with 2 lasagne sheets. Continue with a layer of ricotta mixture and a layer of pasta. Keep layering until all the pasta is used, then finish with a layer of ricotta. Bake in the oven for 30–40 minutes, or until golden. Rest for 15 minutes before serving.

To serve, sauté the rest of the spinach in a little olive oil and scatter it over the top of the lasagne. You may like to add extra dollops of fresh ricotta.

Extravagance
Generosity
Love
/ Tradition
Life
Food

My first mouthful of stuffed artichoke gives me immediate pleasure every time. It is the sort of comfort food I love, as is the classic, bold and robust Sicilian caponata, all sweet and sour on thick, just-grilled slices of chewy sourdough, made by an artisan baker who favors taste and tradition.

For me, my mum's roast lamb with whisky is still the best, most satisfying roast there is. Like many other recipes in this chapter and throughout the book, it typifies my love of herbs and lemons in cooking. Lemons are my son Paul's favorite way of flavoring a dish—especially his roasts, which come pretty close to his grandmother's.

My wife's parents, Palmina and Vincenzo Bertuna, had a remarkable way of chargrilling eggplant and bell peppers, both the red and green varieties, in hot coals on corrugated iron in their backyard. The flavor is earthy, fresh and clean, enriched with good olive oil and seasoning. We all miss their companionship and cooking.

In our family, at the end of a special meal—Easter, Christmas, New Year, a birthday, engagement or wedding, or the introduction of a new girlfriend or boyfriend— cannoli and cassateddi are served with short, strong black coffee. This is life and tradition. It is past and present coming together in appreciation and celebration of great produce and moments of good eating.

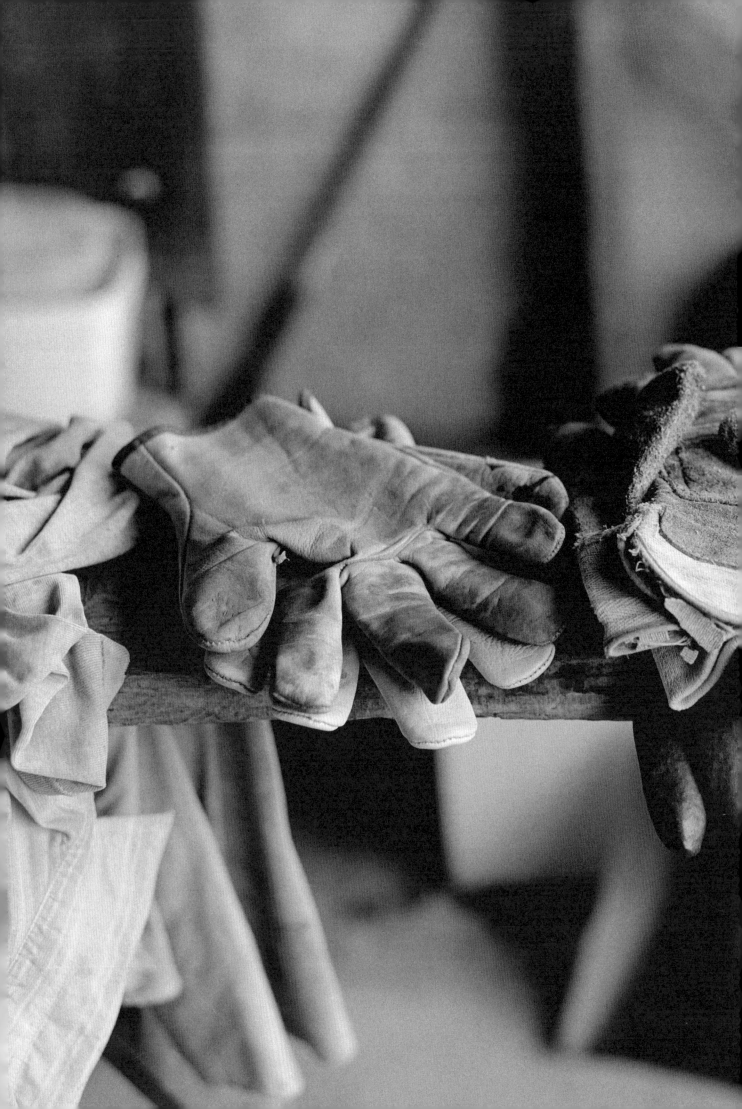

# Roast ocean trout, stuffed Sicilian-style, parsley and fennel salad

I love the way this fish embraces the contrasting flavors of the currant and pine nut stuffing. It is a traditional stuffing that I have used for sardines in the past, but for this recipe I thought, why not stuff a big, fresh, glistening trout for a seductive twist?

Serves 8

1 cup currants
⅓ cup brandy
¾ cup olive oil
2 garlic cloves, finely chopped
2 cups fresh breadcrumbs
½ cup pine nuts, toasted
large handful of parsley, finely chopped
2 teaspoons sugar
salt and freshly ground black pepper
2–3 small sprigs bay leaves (alternatively, use the stems from the fennel)
one 8–9-pound ocean trout, scaled, cleaned and boned by your fishmonger
juice of 1 lemon

SALAD
2 fennel bulbs, thinly sliced
large handful of parsley, torn
2 tablespoons pine nuts, toasted
2 tablespoons extra-virgin olive oil
2 tablespoons verjuice (available in gourmet markets)
salt and freshly ground black pepper

Put the currants in a bowl with the brandy and leave to soften for about 15 minutes.

Preheat the oven to 350°F. Heat 2 tablespoons of the oil in a frying pan and add the garlic, frying gently for 30 seconds without browning. Add the breadcrumbs and fry until light golden, then remove from the heat. Drain the currants (reserving the brandy) and add them to the breadcrumbs with the pine nuts, parsley, sugar and 2 more tablespoons of oil. Season with salt and pepper and stir everything together. Set aside.

Find a roasting dish big enough to accommodate the trout and brush the dish with oil. Lay the bay leaves in the bottom of the dish.

Make sure any traces of blood have been washed from the trout and pat it dry with paper towel. Cut off the fins. Put the trout in the dish and brush it all over with the remaining oil. Season the fish with salt and pepper and stuff the cavity with the breadcrumb mixture. Wrap the tail in foil brushed with oil so it doesn't burn (alternatively, brush the tail itself with a generous amount of oil). Pour the reserved brandy and the lemon juice over the fish and roast uncovered in the oven for 30–40 minutes.

For the salad: toss the ingredients in a bowl, seasoning with salt and pepper.

Rest the cooked trout for 5 minutes before transferring to a serving platter. Cut the trout into slices or, for a more rustic look, break it into pieces with tongs or a knife and fork. Decorate with the bay leaves (they turn a lovely chocolate color in the oven) and serve with the salad.

# Stuffed artichokes

My mother cooks the best stuffed artichokes in the world. They are garlicky and sweet and we have enjoyed them for years. Dad grows his own artichokes, and as they come into flower they are the most stunning plant in his garden. Mum serves her artichokes on a platter with lots of bread to soak up the juices. Who would have thought they would taste so good?

They are also the best accompaniment to homemade wine—somehow the sweetness of the artichokes makes the wine taste better!

Serves 6

3½ cups fresh breadcrumbs
1 cup grated grana padano
1 medium bunch parsley, finely chopped
4–5 thyme sprigs, leaves picked
3 garlic cloves, finely chopped
¾ cup olive oil

salt and freshly ground black pepper
1 lemon, halved
6 large globe artichokes
1 pound ripe tomatoes, skinned, seeded
  and roughly chopped
2 tablespoons butter (optional)

Put the breadcrumbs, grana padano, parsley, thyme, garlic and ¼ cup of the oil in a bowl. Season with salt and pepper. Combine the mixture by rubbing it through your fingers. Set aside.

Fill a small bowl with water and add the juice of half the lemon. Cut off the artichoke stems at the base of the heads. Peel the stems and put them in the water. Tear off just the outer layer of leaves from the artichokes. Cut off the artichoke tops about 1 inch down. Rub all cut surfaces with the other lemon half.

Sit an artichoke upright on your work surface and gently prise open the leaves so you can see into the center. Gently press down to widen the cavity. Use a teaspoon to scoop out the hairy choke in the middle of the artichoke. Season the inside with salt and pepper and fill the gap with stuffing, pressing it down gently with your fingers. Repeat with the other artichokes.

Put the artichokes into a saucepan that will hold them snugly standing upright. Put the stems into the gaps. Scatter the tomatoes over the artichokes and season with salt and pepper. Fill the pot with water to reach halfway up the artichokes and pour over the remaining oil. Dab a little butter (if using) on each artichoke. Cover the pan with a lid and cook on low–medium heat for about 1 hour, or until a leaf from the center of an artichoke is easily plucked out.

To serve, place an artichoke onto a serving plate and drizzle a little of the artichoke water over the top and around the plate.

# Spicy pumpkin caponata bruschetta

Caponata, cannoli and spaghetti with sardines are my family's favorite Sicilian classics. I love the contrasts of the three: the soft creaminess of the Cannoli (page 116) inside the hard but brittle shell of their pastry exterior, the sweet beachy flesh of sardines against the earthiness of wild fennel in Pasta con le Sardi (page 87) and the rich explosion of flavor of the caponata.

I wanted to try something a little different by introducing pumpkin into the mix of ingredients for this bruschetta. Traditionally, caponata has eggplant as its main component, but I adore pumpkin and felt it would do no harm to incorporate it here. Strangely, pumpkin is not a vegetable that is often found in Italian cooking.

Caponata goes well with chicken, meat or fish, but I like it best served with lamb or as part of an antipasto.

Serves 12

½ cup olive oil
1 small onion, finely chopped
1 carrot, finely chopped
1 celery stick, finely chopped
1 garlic clove, finely chopped
1 teaspoon fennel seeds
1 teaspoon ground cumin
1 teaspoon ground coriander
½ teaspoon sumac
½ teaspoon ground ginger
pinch of ground nutmeg
pinch of ground cinnamon
pinch of dried chili flakes
3 thyme sprigs, leaves picked
6 sage leaves
1 tablespoon small capers, rinsed
1 cup black olives
½ cup currants

1 large eggplant, cut into ¾-inch cubes
1 pound pumpkin, peeled and cut into ¾-inch cubes
1 red bell pepper, cut into ¾-inch squares
2¼ pounds ripe tomatoes, skinned, seeded and roughly chopped, or two 14-ounce cans diced Italian tomatoes
2 cups water
salt and freshly ground black pepper
1 teaspoon balsamic vinegar
1 teaspoon sugar
handful of parsley
12 thick slices crusty Italian sourdough
1 garlic clove

Heat the olive oil in a large saucepan over medium heat. Add the onion, carrot and celery and cook until the onion is translucent. Add the garlic and spices and cook for another 2 minutes. Add the herbs, capers, olives, currants, eggplant, pumpkin, bell pepper, tomatoes and water, and season with salt and pepper. Simmer for about 1 hour, partially covered, stirring occasionally. Take off the heat and add the vinegar and sugar and stir through. Adjust the seasoning if needed. Leave to cool a little, then add the parsley.

Toast the bread on the grill of a barbecue, in a chargrill pan or in a regular frying pan. Cut the garlic clove and rub it over the bread as it comes off the heat. Normally I'd drizzle a little extra-virgin olive oil on the bread too, but the caponata is quite rich so it doesn't need it.

Spoon the warm caponata onto the bruschetta and serve.

# Broccoli fritti

This is one of my mum's simplest and tastiest dishes, especially when it's made with Dad's broccoli straight from the garden. Broccoli fritti is terrific on bruschetta or pasta, or with eggs cracked into the pan toward the end of cooking and fried.

Serves 4

2 pounds broccoli
salt and freshly ground black pepper
1 large ripe tomato, skinned, seeded and
   roughly chopped

¾ cup fresh breadcrumbs
2 large garlic cloves, sliced
2 tablespoons grated grana padano
⅓ cup olive oil

Wash the broccoli heads and trim the stems. Cut a cross in the base of each stem. Bring a large pot of water to the boil and add the broccoli heads, stems down. Add 2 tablespoons of salt. As soon as the water comes back to the boil, turn the heads over so the stems are facing up. Cover the pot with a lid and cook for 2–3 minutes, then turn the stems down again. The tiny pin-sized broccoli flowers should have started to open. Cover the pot and cook for another 8 minutes or so. The broccoli should be in the water for a total of 15 minutes and should be just soft.

Drain and cool the broccoli under running water until cool enough to handle. Quarter each head, then chop the quarters into bite-sized pieces. Place in a mixing bowl and season with salt and pepper. Add the tomato, breadcrumbs, garlic and grana padano and toss.

Heat the oil in a heavy-based frying pan until hot. Add the broccoli mixture, spreading it evenly across the pan. If you don't have a large pan it is better to cook this in two batches. Fry the mixture on high heat without stirring until the pieces of broccoli touching the base form a golden crust. Carefully turn the pieces with a spatula (the broccoli will probably break up a little bit) and continue cooking. When the broccoli is crunchy all over and the breadcrumbs are crisp, remove from the heat and serve.

# Roast lamb with whisky

Recently, after all these years, Mum happened to mention the secret to her roast lamb, explaining in an instant why I can never get mine to taste like hers. "Have you put the whisky in?" "Since when have you been adding whisky to your roasts?" "I always add whisky." Some of my mother's recipes can take years to get to know.

This roast has a lovely rustic appearance and looks fantastic on a platter. It goes well with caponata (page 103) or broccoli fritti (page 104).

Serves 12

6-pound leg and loin of lamb in one piece
juice and rind of 1 lemon
1 cup olive oil
salt and freshly ground black pepper
5 garlic cloves, finely sliced
5 rosemary sprigs, leaves picked

4 oregano sprigs, leaves picked
1 large onion, finely chopped
1 large carrot, finely chopped
2 celery sticks, finely chopped
1 cup whisky

Preheat the oven to 475°F. Place the lamb on a large baking sheet. Pour the lemon juice and half the oil over the lamb and season with plenty of salt and pepper. Massage the mixture into the lamb, including inside the loin.

Make shallow cuts all over the surface of the lamb and stuff these with garlic, rosemary, oregano and pieces of lemon rind. Also scatter these ingredients inside the loin. Tie the loin together with kitchen string.

Move the lamb aside and place the onion, carrot and celery on the baking sheet. Put the lamb back on top and pour over the remaining oil and the whisky. Place the baking sheet in the oven.

Roast for 15–20 minutes, then turn the temperature down to 400°F and roast for about 1 hour. Remove the lamb from the oven and cover with several layers of foil and tea towels to keep warm and rest for 30 minutes.

Cut the string from the lamb and carve the meat. Spoon the fat out of the pan juices and serve the meat with the juices and vegetables on top.

# Eggplant parmigiana

There are so many versions of this dish made by and loved by Italians everywhere that at a recent Mirabella reunion there seemed to be a different *melanzane alla parmigiana* on every table, all of them beautiful. The one that I make was taught to me by my mother-in-law, Palmina Bertuna, who would add a layer of caramelized onion with breadcrumbs. Like my mum's recipe, beaten eggs are used for binding the layers, as well as grated cheese.

Serves 8

TOMATO SAUCE
⅓ cup olive oil
1 onion, finely chopped
1 carrot, finely chopped
1 celery stick, finely chopped
pinch of dried chili flakes (optional)
2 garlic cloves, finely chopped
6 pounds ripe tomatoes, roughly chopped
1 bay leaf
½ bunch basil, leaves picked
2 thyme sprigs
1 teaspoon sugar
salt and freshly ground black pepper
½ cup butter

2 medium eggplants
salt
⅔ cup olive oil
3 medium onions, finely sliced
    into rounds
4 cups fresh breadcrumbs, plus
    a handful extra
4 eggs
freshly ground black pepper
1 cup grated grana padano

For the sauce: heat the oil in a heavy-based saucepan. Add the onion, carrot, celery and chili flakes (if using) and cook until the onion is translucent. Add the garlic and cook for 30 seconds without browning, then add the tomatoes and cover the pan with a lid. Bring to the boil, then turn the heat back to a simmer. Cook, partially covered, for 45–60 minutes.
*Continued*

# Eggplant parmigiana
## (continued)

Press the sauce through a food mill to remove the tomato skins and seeds and return the sauce to the pot. Add the bay leaf, basil, thyme and sugar and season with salt and pepper. Simmer for another 30 minutes uncovered. Remove from the heat, take out the bay leaf and stir in the butter.

Slice the eggplants into ¼-inch discs. Lightly salt the slices on both sides and layer them between pieces of paper towel. Leave for a few minutes. Heat half the oil in a heavy-based frying pan and fry a few eggplant slices at a time until golden brown on both sides. Drain the cooked slices on paper towel.

In the same pan, heat the rest of the oil and gently fry the onions until golden brown. Add the 4 cups breadcrumbs and cook, stirring constantly, for 4–5 minutes. The onion flavor should be through the breadcrumbs, and they should start to toast.

Preheat the oven to 350°F. Butter a deep casserole dish. Sprinkle the handful of extra bread-crumbs into the dish and shake off any excess. Crack the eggs into a bowl, season with salt and pepper, and lightly beat with a fork.

Cover the bottom of the dish with a ladleful of sauce. Arrange eggplant slices over the sauce. Add a layer of onion and breadcrumbs, then spoon over some egg. Press down lightly. Add more sauce and sprinkle on some grana padano. Repeat these layers, finishing with layers of sauce and cheese. Bake in the oven for 45 minutes, until golden.

Rest the parmigiana for 15 minutes before serving (or you can serve it at room temperature). If you have used a dish without a lip, you can run a knife around it, place a plate over the top and turn it upside down as if you were getting a cake out, then turn the parmigiana right-side up onto a serving plate. Otherwise, leave it in the dish and cut it into slices or simply scoop out servings.

# Chicken, bell peppers and leek couscous

Couscous, or *cuscus* as it is known in Sicily, is a classic example of the Arab contribution to the diverse mix of cultures that have blended and mingled on the island over the centuries, including the Greeks, Normans, French, Spanish and Italians. My parents' village of Calatafimi is only forty-five minutes from the famous Trapani fish market, where, as Robert Freson writes in his book *Savoring Italy*, you will find the best example of couscous, served with fish in summer and meat in winter. Freson notes that couscous is steamed semolina, "the flavor of which depends solely on the richness of the broth in which the semolina is steamed."

Serves 4

½ cup olive oil
¾ cup butter
1 small onion, finely chopped
1 small carrot, finely chopped
1 celery stick, finely chopped
pinch of dried chili flakes
1 leek (white part only), sliced into thin discs
2 tablespoons tomato paste
grated zest of 1 lemon
6 thyme sprigs
2 garlic cloves, finely chopped
2 large red bell peppers, sliced into thin strips

3 free-range chicken breasts, skin off, cut into
    bite-sized pieces
1 cup dry white wine
2 cups chicken stock
9 ounces couscous
1 cup black olives
1 cup grated grana padano
1 medium bunch parsley, finely chopped
salt and freshly ground black pepper
herbs to garnish such as parsley or thyme
    leaves, or chopped chives or spring onions

Heat the oil and ½ cup of the butter in a large heavy-based saucepan. Add the onion, carrot, celery and chili flakes, and cook until the onion is translucent. Add the leek, tomato paste, lemon zest, thyme, garlic and bell peppers and cook until the leek and bell peppers have softened.

Add the chicken and brown the pieces all over. Pour in the wine and cook until almost completely reduced, then add the stock and bring to the boil. Add the couscous, stirring everything together. Remove from the heat and stir in the olives, grana padano, parsley and remaining butter. Season with salt and pepper. Cover with a lid and leave to rest for 5 minutes. The couscous will absorb all the liquid. Stir again and serve garnished with herbs.

# Chargrilled lamb, eggplant, tomato and feta salad

My mother-in-law, Palmina, used to cook bell peppers in the embers of a fire, which she would make in the middle of a clearing in her husband Vincenzo's vegetable garden. Using a piece of cardboard, she would fan the embers in order to char the skins, which gave the flesh its delicious, distinctive chargrilled flavor. While the bell peppers were still warm, she would rub the skins off in her apron, tear the flesh into strips and place them in a bowl with olive oil and garlic, salt and freshly ground pepper. It was perfect on crusty Italian bread or served with grilled steak or chicken. The eggplant and tomatoes in this recipe are prepared in the same way. If you're unable to build a fire in your backyard, use the grill of a barbecue, brushing it with olive oil first.

Serves 8

4½ pounds lamb backstraps
½ cup olive oil
3 garlic cloves, finely chopped
4 parsley sprigs, finely chopped
3 rosemary sprigs, leaves picked
1 teaspoon fennel seeds
pinch of dried chili flakes
salt and freshly ground black pepper

4 medium eggplants
8 ripe tomatoes
½ cup extra-virgin olive oil
1 garlic clove, crushed
salt and freshly ground black pepper
handful of young basil leaves
handful of parsley
4 ounces feta

Trim the lamb backstraps of any fat and cut them in half widthwise. Combine the oil, garlic, parsley, rosemary, fennel seeds and chili flakes in a large bowl and season with salt and pepper. Add the lamb, massaging the marinade into the meat. Leave to marinate for at least 1 hour or ideally in the refrigerator overnight (but bring the meat back to room temperature before cooking).

Prepare a fire, burning enough wood to provide a decent amount of charcoal. Place the eggplants and tomatoes straight on the coals. Fan the coals occasionally to create more heat. As the skins of the eggplants and tomatoes start to blister, turn them gently. Continue this process until the skins are scorched all over. Remove from the coals and place in a dish to cool a little. Peel the tomatoes and eggplants, leaving the eggplant stems intact (and tomato stems if they have them), and set aside.

If you have a cast-iron barbecue plate that will fit over your fire, stoke the fire and heat the plate. Otherwise, heat the grill of a barbecue and brush it with olive oil. Cook the lamb for 8–10 minutes on each side for medium–rare, or until cooked to your liking. Take the lamb off the heat, cover with foil and rest in a warm place for 20 minutes.

As a dressing, combine the extra-virgin olive oil and garlic in a small bowl, seasoning with salt and pepper. Arrange the whole eggplants and tomatoes on a large platter. Slice the lamb backstraps diagonally and lay the meat over the eggplants and tomatoes. Scatter with basil and parsley leaves and crumble feta over the top. Drizzle with the dressing and serve.

# Sausages and lentils, mixed mushrooms, chili and dill mascarpone

Where I live, on the Mornington Peninsula, it is difficult to find good Italian sausages. There is nothing like authentic pork and fennel sausages cooked this way with lovely rustic lentils. The addition of the mascarpone is just a bit of fun and isn't necessary, though I do like the way it cuts through the strong flavor of the sausages. Mum and Dad wouldn't approve of this at all!

Serves 4

½ cup olive oil
1 small onion, finely chopped
1 carrot, finely chopped
1 celery stick, finely chopped
8 sausages such as Italian pork and
    fennel or chicken
1 garlic clove, finely chopped
1 small red chili, finely sliced
8 ripe tomatoes, skinned, seeded and
    roughly chopped, or two 14-ounce cans
    diced Italian tomatoes
⅔ pound green lentils, soaked overnight
6 cups boiling water
salt and freshly ground black pepper

MASCARPONE
½ pound mascarpone
1 long red chili, finely sliced diagonally
4 dill sprigs, finely chopped

MUSHROOMS
⅓ cup olive oil
4 tablespoons butter
1 pound mixed mushrooms, such as cremini,
    shiitake and enoki, trimmed
dash of white wine
2 garlic cloves, finely chopped
grated zest of 1 small lemon
4 thyme sprigs, leaves picked
salt and freshly ground black pepper

Heat the oil in a large heavy-based saucepan. Add the onion, carrot and celery and cook gently until the onion is translucent. Add the sausages and brown them all over. Add the garlic, chili and tomatoes, stirring well, then add the lentils. Cover with a lid and cook gently for 10 minutes. Add the boiling water, cover again and simmer for about 45 minutes, until the lentils are tender. Taste for seasoning and add salt and pepper if needed.

For the mascarpone: mix the mascarpone, chili and dill together in a bowl.

For the mushrooms: heat the oil and butter in a heavy-based saucepan and add the mushrooms (except the enoki, if using). Don't stir them constantly; let them brown a little, then shake the pan or stir gently and leave them alone again for a while. This way they end up with a crunchier texture. When nicely browned, add the dash of wine and the garlic and cook until the mushrooms have absorbed the liquid. Remove from the heat and add the lemon zest, thyme and enoki mushrooms (if using). Season with salt and pepper.

To serve, spoon the sausages and lentils onto warm plates. Top with the mushrooms and a dollop of mascarpone.

# Cardoons and cauliflower in batter

Cardoons and cauliflower have a sweet flavor in late autumn and early winter—it's the beginning of the season and they are ready to be eaten. Cardoon plants look like a small celery with a crown of silvery gray leaves. They are closely related to the artichoke and have a similar flavor, but are a little bitter. Both the cardoon and the artichoke are quintessentially Sicilian. My father plants his cardoons in mid-summer, caring for them with plenty of chicken manure and water; in late autumn he covers the stems with hessian or straw and keeps up the watering, which keeps the stems tender and sweet.

Sicilians have been battering and frying vegetables for centuries in a way that's not unlike Japanese tempura. You can parboil just about any vegetables and prepare them in this way. They're a great snack to have with beer.

Serves 4

6 cardoon bunches
1 cauliflower
salt
3½ cups all-purpose flour
½ cup grated grana padano

large handful of parsley, finely chopped
4 garlic cloves, crushed
freshly ground black pepper
2½ cups water
olive oil for frying

Pull off the tough outer stalks of the cardoons and discard. Cut the bunches off at the base to separate the remaining stalks, and set the tender hearts aside for another use, such as pasta or frittata. Trim the leaves and spikes from the stalks and de-string the outside surfaces. Turn the stalks over and, working from the top, either peel away the inside skin or scrape it off with a knife. Be careful not to remove too much—you only need to remove one layer. Cut the stalks diagonally into 4-inch lengths, pulling away any additional string as you go.

Cut the cauliflower into quarters. Cut each quarter into thick, flat slices.

Cook the cardoons in a pot of salted boiling water until tender, then remove with a slotted spoon and drain. Add the cauliflower to the water and cook until tender, and drain.

Combine the flour, grana padano, parsley and garlic in a bowl and season with salt and pepper. Gradually add the water, mixing well with a fork.

Pour ¾ inch olive oil into a deep-sided frying pan and heat. After a while, test the temperature by adding a drop of batter—when it bubbles and begins to brown, the oil is hot enough. Set the heat to medium, then dip pieces of cardoon and cauliflower in batter and fry in batches until light golden, turning them over halfway through. Remove from the oil and drain on paper towel while you fry more. You may need to add more oil, or even change it if it gets very dirty.

Serve the cardoons and cauliflower as soon as they have drained, or wait until everything is fried and pile it onto a platter and serve as quickly as possible.

# Prosciutto and cherry tomato bruschetta

Bruschetta is terrific served with drinks before dinner. Keep it simple, using the best sourdough bread available, the ripest, freshest tomatoes you can find and your favorite extra-virgin olive oil.

Serves 4

4 thick slices crusty Italian sourdough
1 garlic clove
⅓ cup extra-virgin olive oil
salt and freshly ground black pepper
1 pound trussed cherry tomatoes, separated but still with their stems
8 slices prosciutto

Toast the bread on the grill of a barbecue, in a chargrill pan or in a regular frying pan. Cut the garlic clove and rub it over one side of the bread as the slices come off the heat. Pour the oil on a plate and season with salt and lots of pepper. Press each garlic-rubbed side of toast into the oil and place the slices on a serving platter. Take the tomatoes in your hands and gently squeeze them over the bruschetta so that their seeds and juice pool on top of the toasted bread. Arrange the prosciutto on top of the bruschetta and serve.

# Cannoli

Every one of my aunts has her own version of this classic Sicilian dessert, although I love Mum's the best. She always puts a tiny piece of dark chocolate in the ends of her cannoli, and I've added chopped nuts for something more baroque. These are great with strong black coffee.

You will need metal cannoli tubes, which can be purchased from good Italian delis, or you can use dried cannelloni pasta tubes, which you will have to throw away at the end.

Makes about 16 cannoli

PASTRY
¼ cup white wine
1 tablespoon olive oil
1 tablespoon sugar
2 cups all-purpose flour
2 eggs, separated (whites lightly beaten)

4½ cups canola oil
confectioners' sugar to serve

FILLING
1 pound ricotta, drained overnight in a sieve set over a bowl in the refrigerator
3 tablespoons superfine sugar
grated zest of 1 small lemon
2 tablespoons chopped or grated dark chocolate
handful of pistachios, chopped
handful of hazelnuts, chopped
grated zest of 1 orange

For the pastry: bring the wine, oil and sugar to a boil in a small saucepan, stirring until the sugar dissolves. Set aside to cool.

Tip the flour onto a work surface and make a well in the center. Pour the egg yolks and wine mixture into the well and gradually incorporate into the flour with your fingers. Bring the mixture together into a dough and knead for 5 minutes.

Cut the dough into 4 even pieces. Roll each piece into an oval shape, then pass through a pasta machine at its widest setting. Fold in half and put it through again—do this about 10 times, until the pastry is smooth. Now roll the pastry through on the second-last notch. Place the sheet on an unfloured bench and roll out the remaining dough using the same method.

Cut circles in the pastry sheets measuring 3½–4 inches in diameter and wrap these around the cannoli tubes. Seal the edges with a little of the beaten egg white, trying not to get any on the metal tubes as it will stick and make it difficult to slide the cannoli off once they're cooked.

Pour the canola oil into a saucepan—there should be enough for the cannoli shells to float. Heat gently, testing the temperature by adding a small piece of pastry—when it bubbles and begins to brown, turn the heat down to low. Fry 3 or 4 shells at a time, turning them over as the sides become a light golden color. When golden all over, place them on paper towel to drain. Wrap the tubes with more pastry, continuing this process until you have used all the circles. Roll the scraps of dough through the pasta machine to make more cannoli.

For the filling: combine the ricotta, superfine sugar and lemon zest in a bowl and stir with a fork until smooth. Combine the chocolate, nuts and orange zest in a flat dish. Just before serving, fill each cannoli shell with the ricotta, pushing it down with a small spoon or a knife, then dip one or both ends into the chocolate mixture—a little should stick to the filling. Arrange the cannoli on a platter and dust with confectioners' sugar.

# Cassateddi

Cassateddi are my mother's special dessert, made for Easter and Christmas, much to everyone's joy. They are like the jewel at the end of a meal—beautiful, warm parcels of sweetened ricotta to have with coffee. The ingredients are similar to those used in cannoli.

Makes about 16 cassateddi

PASTRY
¼ cup white wine
1 tablespoon olive oil
1 tablespoon sugar
1¼ cups all-purpose flour
2 eggs, separated (whites lightly beaten)

1 quart canola oil
confectioners' sugar to serve

FILLING
7 ounces ricotta, drained overnight in a sieve
    set over a bowl in the refrigerator
2 tablespoons superfine sugar
2 teaspoons grated dark chocolate
grated zest of 1 small lemon
few gratings of fresh nutmeg or a pinch
    of ground nutmeg

For the pastry: bring the wine, olive oil and sugar to a boil in a small saucepan, stirring until the sugar dissolves. Set aside to cool.

Tip the flour onto a work surface and make a well in the center. Pour the egg yolks and wine mixture into the well and gradually incorporate into the flour with your fingers. Bring the mixture together to form a dough.

Cut the dough into 2 even pieces. Roll each piece into an oval shape. Then pass through a pasta machine at its widest setting. Fold in half and put it through again—do this about 10 times, until the pastry is smooth. Now roll the pastry through on the second-last notch. Place the sheet on an unfloured bench and roll out the remaining dough.

For the filling: combine the filling ingredients in a bowl, stirring with a fork until smooth.

Cut circles in the pastry sheets measuring 3½–4 inches in diameter. Spoon a tablespoon of filling onto a side of each circle. Brush a little of the beaten egg white around the rim and fold the pastry over. Seal by pressing down on the edges with your fingers, or use a fork to create a ridged effect.

Roll the scraps of dough through the pasta machine and cut more circles to make more cassateddi. Prick each with a toothpick before frying to allow air to escape.

Put the canola oil in a saucepan—there should be enough for the turnovers to float, so you may need to add a little more. Begin to heat, testing the temperature after a while by adding a small piece of pastry—when it bubbles and begins to brown, scoop it out and turn the heat down to low. Fry 4 or 5 turnovers at a time, turning them over as the sides become puffed and golden. When golden all over, remove from the oil and place on paper towel to drain while you cook another batch. Toss the drained turnovers in superfine sugar and serve while hot, or keep them warm until all of them are ready. If you want to make cassateddi in advance, you can reheat them in a low oven.

Extravagance
Generosity
Love
Tradition
/ Life
Food

Why have I included these recipes in a chapter called Life? They are dishes that I love to eat, I feel connected to and could never go without.

Nonna's fish soup that healed me whenever I was ill. My mother's minestrone that fed me well when I was hungry and there was nothing else to eat. My daughter Pam's bruschetta, which celebrates and blends all that is Italian. My son Paul's favorite chicken salad, except hold the tomatoes (the boy has always had a problem with that most Mediterranean of ingredients; you've got to love him though). My daughter Danielle adores rhubarb, like I do, and her food, like I do, and is the best shopper ever! Rosa and her almond biscotti that go so well with an espresso. Rosa is like a true sister—earthy and romantic, funny, confident and strong. Merle Kingston, who came into our lives at the café and whose spirit and zest for life fill so much of the place. Her roulade lives on. Year after year, my father has been growing cavulisceddi in his garden for us to eat— no one grows it better than Dad. And I will never forget all those years ago sitting at my girlfriend Johanne's family table with my future in-laws surrounding me, and in the center of the table Jo's trifle, splendid in yellow, cream, green, pink and red. And it's still as wonderfully delicate and full of surprises today, even after all these years!

# Chargrilled chicken and vegetable salad

Variations of this salad have been on our café menu from the first day we opened. It is a good example of how simply prepared ingredients such as spinach leaves, chargrilled vegetables and beautifully cooked chicken can form a delicious combination. Instead of chicken, you could use chargrilled lamb or beef. If you don't want to use meat, add potatoes, boiled or roasted, or even pumpkin and chickpeas. Simple and satisfying.

Serves 6

4 free-range chicken breasts, skin on
zest and juice of 1 lemon
⅔ cup olive oil
salt and freshly ground black pepper
1 medium eggplant, thinly sliced lengthwise
3 small zucchini, thinly sliced lengthwise
12 asparagus spears, ends trimmed
1 red bell pepper
6 artichoke hearts in oil, drained and halved

12 snow peas, topped, tailed and strung,
    cut lengthwise into strips
1 pound cherry tomatoes, halved
1 cup black or green olives
4–5 handfuls of baby spinach leaves
    or watercress
2 oregano sprigs, leaves picked
1 teaspoon balsamic vinegar
¼ cup extra-virgin olive oil

Put the chicken breasts in a bowl and add the lemon zest and juice and half the olive oil. Season with salt and pepper and rub the mixture into the meat. Marinate in the refrigerator for about 1 hour.

Preheat the oven to 400°F. Heat the grill of a barbecue or a chargrill pan and cook the chicken until charred on both sides. Transfer to a baking sheet and roast in the oven for 15–20 minutes or until cooked through. Remove from the oven and set aside to cool to room temperature.

Put the eggplant, zucchini and asparagus in a bowl and drizzle with the remaining oil. Season with salt and pepper.

Place the bell pepper on the barbecue grill or in the chargrill pan and cook until blackened all over. Set aside to cool while you grill the eggplant, zucchini and asparagus. Tear the grilled eggplant slices in half. Peel the bell pepper, discard the seeds and cut or tear the flesh into thin strips.

Discard the chicken skin and shred the meat with your fingers. Put it into a mixing bowl and pour over any juices from the baking sheet. Add the bell pepper, eggplant, zucchini and asparagus as well as the artichoke hearts, snow peas, tomatoes, olives, spinach and oregano. Drizzle with the vinegar and extra-virgin olive oil. Gently toss with your hands and arrange on a serving platter.

# Nonna's fish soup

My Nonna loved this soup, and believed it could cure ailments—from colds to rheumatism and backaches—and would always put a smile on your face. If she was unable to purchase fish from the fishmonger's carriage in the street, Nonna would trick her children and call this soup *brodu cu lu pisci scappatu* (soup with the fish that got away). They never suspected a thing. Try it without the fish—it's surprisingly fishy!

Serves 4

4 garlic cloves, peeled
4 parsley sprigs, leaves picked, plus extra
    chopped parsley to serve
2 dill sprigs, leaves picked, plus extra chopped
    dill to serve
½ bunch chives, chopped, plus extra to serve
salt
¼ cup olive oil
5 ripe tomatoes, skinned, seeded and roughly
    chopped, or two 14.5 ounce cans diced
    Italian tomatoes

1 bay leaf
6 cups water
one 2-pound whole white-fleshed fish such as
    flathead or snapper, scaled and cleaned
freshly ground black pepper
7 ounces vermicelli pasta, broken into
    2⅓-inch lengths

Pound the garlic, parsley, dill, chives and a pinch of salt to a paste using a mortar and pestle.

Heat the oil in a heavy-based pot and gently fry the paste for 1–2 minutes, until the garlic becomes light golden. Add the tomatoes and bay leaf and fry for another 5 minutes. Add the water and bring to the boil, then simmer for 15 minutes.

Cut off the head, tail and fins from the fish and put them in the pot. Simmer for another 20 minutes. Chop the remaining fish into large pieces, cutting through the bones, and add to the pot, simmering for another 10 minutes. Season the soup with salt and pepper.

Meanwhile, cook the pasta in a pot of salted boiling water until al dente. Drain thoroughly and return to its pot. Remove the fish pieces from the soup, discarding the head, tail and fins. Strain the broth into the pot with the pasta. Remove the fish flesh from the bones and add to the pot. Warm the soup for 1 minute and serve with chopped parsley, dill and chives.

# Pistachio and herb-crumbed chicken breasts

*Cotoletta di pollo*, or crumbed chicken, is my version of schnitzel, where chicken breasts are coated in a chunky mixture of nuts, herbs and breadcrumbs. I also use this mix to stuff chicken breasts, and usually add onions, bacon, dates or currants and sometimes dried apricots. It's a pleasing combination of many foods and flavors I love to eat.

Serves 4

4 free-range chicken breasts, skin off
⅓ cup pistachios, finely chopped
1 teaspoon finely chopped rosemary
10 sage leaves, finely chopped
1 garlic clove, finely chopped
½ cup grated pecorino or grana padano

grated zest of 1 lemon
2 cups fresh breadcrumbs
salt and freshly ground black pepper
2 eggs
¼ cup olive oil
lemon wedges

Gently pound the chicken breasts at their thickest ends with a mallet or rolling pin to make them an even thickness all over.

Combine the nuts, rosemary, sage, garlic, pecorino, lemon zest and breadcrumbs in a bowl and season with salt and pepper. Mix thoroughly.

Lightly beat the eggs in another bowl. Coat each chicken breast in egg and then in the breadcrumb mixture, pressing it down so the mixture sticks evenly over the meat. Refrigerate the crumbed breasts for about 1 hour.

Heat the oil in a frying pan over medium heat and cook the chicken until brown on both sides. Drain on paper towel and serve with the lemon wedges.

# Pam's bruschetta—sausages, tomatoes, olives, bocconcini

Pam is the second of our three children; she is our middle child. She is named after Johanne's mother, Palmina Bertuna, also known as Palmina La Fayette. Pam is definitely of an Italian spirit: generous and womanly, fiercely independent and loyal, wielding a certain power within the dynamics of our family that is only matched by her mother.

This bruschetta was prepared by Pam at a time when she was working back-of-house in our café. It combines ingredients and flavors that are robust, imaginative and classic, a celebration of all that is Italian.

Serves 8

4 Italian sausages
¼ cup olive oil
2 garlic cloves; 1 finely chopped, 1 whole
4 dill sprigs, leaves picked
salt and freshly ground black pepper
4 ripe tomatoes, quartered
large handful of basil leaves

2 handfuls of arugula
½ cup black olives
8 bocconcini balls, torn
8 anchovies
¼ cup extra-virgin olive oil
8 thick slices crusty Italian sourdough

Cut the sausages in half lengthwise and put them in a dish. Add the olive oil, chopped garlic and dill and season with a little salt and pepper. Stir the sausages around to ensure they are well coated. Leave to marinate while you combine the tomatoes, basil, arugula, olives, bocconcini, anchovies and extra-virgin olive oil in a separate bowl, season with salt and pepper.

Heat the grill of a barbecue, a chargrill pan or a regular frying pan and cook the sausages. Wipe the cooking surface clean and toast the bread. Cut the whole garlic clove and rub it over one side of the bread as the slices come off the heat. Top the bruschetta with the grilled sausages and salad and serve.

# Roast duck, wilted cavulisceddi

Cavulisceddi, or broccoli rape, has a similar flavor to tender young radish leaves. It can be purchased from good Italian greengrocers but, better still, grow your own. The seeds can be bought from Italian delicatessens. My father grows this vegetable so that it is ready to eat at the beginning of autumn. If you can't get cavulisceddi, you can use chicory or any other bitter green.

Serves 4

two 4-pound ducks
⅔ cup olive oil
salt and freshly ground black pepper
2 lemons, quartered
2 tablespoons finely chopped ginger
2 garlic cloves, roughly crushed with the side
   of a knife
4 rosemary sprigs
½ cup butter
½ cup honey

CAVULISCEDDI
2 tablespoons olive oil
2 teaspoons balsamic vinegar
1 garlic clove, finely sliced
1 bunch broccoli rape (about 1 pound),
   cut in half and any thick stems sliced
salt and freshly ground black pepper

Preheat the oven to 400°F. Cut off the duck necks and wing tips and discard. Pull off the oil glands on either side of the tail (they feel like small beans and are covered with a membrane), as well as any other excess fatty bits. Wash the ducks inside and out and pat dry.

Pour the oil over the ducks and into their cavities and season inside and out with salt and pepper. Rub the mixture into the skin. Put the lemon quarters, ginger, garlic, rosemary and half the butter into the cavities. Smear the remaining butter and the honey over the breasts. Put the ducks on a baking sheet breast-side down and roast for 1 hour until golden brown. Remove from the oven, cover with foil and keep warm while you prepare the cavulisceddi.

For the cavulisceddi: heat the oil and vinegar in a frying pan then add the garlic and broccoli rape. Cover with a lid and cook for 2–3 minutes, or until the leaves start to wilt. Season with salt and pepper and serve alongside the duck.

# Minestrone

This thick, warm and chunky dish is not a light soup. It's Mum's version, and her secret star ingredient is Swiss chard. A good soup sums up all that you need in life: it gives pleasure to the heart and cures crankiness, which can be essential during the long winter months.

Serves 8

⅔ cup olive oil
1 medium onion, finely chopped
½ teaspoon dried chili flakes
½ cup each of dried kidney beans, cannellini beans, borlotti beans, chickpeas and lentils, soaked together in a bowl overnight
1 carrot, finely chopped
1 large potato, peeled and diced into ½-inch cubes
½ small cauliflower, cut into small florets
3 celery sticks, finely sliced
½ bunch Swiss chard, stalks finely sliced, leaves chopped and reserved

2 pounds ripe tomatoes, skinned, seeded and roughly chopped, or two 14-ounce cans diced Italian tomatoes
5 quarts water
⅓ pound short pasta (or spaghetti broken into 1-inch lengths)
½ pound broccoli, cut into small florets
1 medium zucchini, cut into ⅓-inch cubes
⅔ pound shelled peas, fresh or frozen
salt and freshly ground black pepper
grated grana padano to serve

Heat the oil in a large heavy-based pot and gently fry the onion and chili for 2 minutes. Add the soaked beans, chickpeas and lentils along with the carrot, potato, cauliflower, celery, Swiss chard stalks and tomatoes. Cover with a lid and cook gently for about 10 minutes, stirring occasionally.

Add the water, cover again and bring to the boil. Turn the heat down to low–medium and cook for another 1¾ hours, partially covered.

Meanwhile, cook the pasta in a pot of salted boiling water until al dente. Drain and reserve 1 cup of the cooking water.

Add the Swiss chard leaves, the broccoli, zucchini and peas to the soup and cook for 5 minutes more. Add the pasta and cooking water and season with salt and pepper. Serve topped with grana padano.

# Banana and honey roulade, ginger custard

My friend Merle Kingston brought this lovely old-fashioned dessert to the café and it's another dish that has stayed on the menu for years. Neither of us are trained chefs but Merle's guidance, determination and love of food and cooking have improved my life and my little café, for which I'm sure my customers are grateful.

Serves 8–10

1¼ cups cream
1½ tablespoons honey, plus more to serve
2 bananas, peeled and sliced
1 cup superfine sugar, plus extra for coating
 baking sheet
6–7 egg whites
pinch of salt

confectioners' sugar (optional) to serve

GINGER CUSTARD
1 cup milk
⅓-inch piece ginger, peeled
½ vanilla bean, split
3 egg yolks
⅓ cup superfine sugar

Whip the cream. When it begins to thicken, drizzle in the honey and continue whipping until the cream is stiff. Add the bananas, churning them into the cream. Refrigerate.

Spray the inside of a 13-by-9-inch baking dish with oil spray. Line the base and sides with parchment paper and leave some paper hanging over the edges. Spray more oil over the paper and sprinkle on some sugar, coating the paper well. Shake out any excess.

Preheat the oven to 350°F. Put ¾ cup of the superfine sugar, the egg whites and salt in a mixing bowl and beat with electric beaters for about 6 minutes until stiff and glossy. Pour into the baking sheet and spread evenly. Bake for about 10 minutes, until lightly golden. Set aside to cool completely.

For the custard: put the milk, ginger and vanilla bean in a saucepan and heat gently, almost to boiling point. Whisk the egg yolks and sugar in a bowl and slowly pour in the hot milk (including the ginger and vanilla), whisking constantly. Wipe out the saucepan and pour the mixture back in. Place over low heat and stir until it thickens enough to coat the back of a spoon. Strain the custard and keep warm.

Keeping the meringue on its baking sheet, peel the edges of paper away from the sides of meringue. Spread the banana cream on top. Place a long serving plate next to the tray and partially lift the meringue onto the plate by dragging it with the paper. Fold the lip of paper beneath the meringue sitting on the plate. Roll the meringue around the banana cream, starting from the end still in the baking sheet. You need to roll up and over the edge of the tray. The meringue roulade should be rolled off the paper and baking sheet and onto the plate in one movement.

Drizzle the roulade with extra honey and dust with confectioners' sugar, if desired. Serve slices of roulade with the ginger custard.

# Apricot tart

Another of my friend Merle's recipes, this is the simplest and one of the most delicious desserts there is. I love cooked apricots, but you could also use fresh juicy figs—just break them in half and place them on top instead of the apricots. Or you might wish to use fresh berries such as strawberries, or blueberries, raspberries or a combination of all three.

Serves 8

1 ¼ cups self-rising flour
¾ cup superfine sugar
¼ cup almond meal
¾ cup butter, softened
1 teaspoon vanilla extract
3 eggs
1 apple, peeled and grated
8 ripe apricots, halved
confectioners' sugar to serve
heavy cream to serve

Preheat the oven to 350°F. Butter and flour a 4⅓-by-13-inch rectangular tart pan with a removable base (or use a round pan if you don't have a rectangular one).

Place all ingredients except the apricots in a mixing bowl and beat with electric beaters for 3–4 minutes, until the mixture becomes pale. Spread in the tart pan and scatter the apricot halves over the top, cut-side up. Bake in the oven until golden brown. Cool and remove from the pan. Dust with confectioners' sugar and serve with heavy cream.

# Rhubarb and strawberry crostata

This *crostata* (tart) goes against tradition in that it is not made in a pan. It has a free-form, rustic appearance and is especially delicious served warm with sweet mascarpone, as described here, or if you like, you could serve it with sour cream or ice cream. Yum! Yum! Yum!

Serves 8–10

SOUR CREAM PASTRY
1 cup chilled butter, chopped
2 cups all-purpose flour
½ cup sour cream

FILLING
6 large rhubarb stalks, sliced diagonally into
   ¾–1-inch pieces
1 pound strawberries, hulled
¾ cup superfine sugar
2 tablespoons custard powder
grated zest of 1 lemon

MASCARPONE
1 pound mascarpone
grated zest of 1 lemon
1 tablespoon confectioners' sugar

1 egg yolk

For the pastry: pulse the butter and flour in a food processor until the mixture resembles breadcrumbs. Add the sour cream and pulse until the dough just forms a ball. Wrap the dough in plastic wrap and refrigerate for 20 minutes.

For the filling: combine all the ingredients in a large bowl and toss well.

For the mascarpone: in a bowl, stir together the mascarpone, lemon zest and confectioners' sugar.

Preheat the oven to 400°F. On a floured surface, roll the pastry out to a rough circle around ¼ inch thick and 1½ inches wide. Place on a tray lined with parchment paper. Pile the filling into the center of the pastry and spread it out, leaving about a 1½ inch edge. Turn the edges over the filling and brush them with the egg yolk. Bake the crostata in the oven until the pastry is golden, around 45 minutes to 1 hour.

Serve straight from the oven topped with the sweet mascarpone and with more fresh strawberries, if you desire.

# Rosa's almond biscotti

Rosa's almond biscotti are displayed on our counter on Mondays and Saturdays. Those are the days Rosa, my sister, manages to squeeze cooking for the café into her busy week while raising Sophie and "the twins," Francesca and Marcella, as well as feeding Michael and conducting her popular cooking classes. These biscotti make a lot of people happy, just like Rosa.

Makes about 20

2⅓ cups almond meal
1 cup superfine sugar
3 egg whites
grated zest of 1 orange
2 teaspoons almond extract
2 cups flaked almonds
2 tablespoons confectioners' sugar

Preheat the oven to 350°F. Combine the almond meal, sugar, egg whites, orange zest and almond extract in a bowl, stirring well. Put the flaked almonds in a separate bowl.

Roll a tablespoon of biscotti mixture into a rough ball, then roll the ball in flaked almonds. With your thumb, forefinger and middle finger, pinch the ball into a rough pyramid shape. Stand it up on a tray lined with parchment paper and continue making balls until all the mixture is used.

Bake the biscotti in the oven for 10–12 minutes, or until light golden. Leave to cool, then dust with the confectioners' sugar. Store in an airtight container.

# Berry and rhubarb trifle

Trifle is my favorite dessert ever! It doesn't matter how many versions there are, I love them all—jelly ones, pineapple ones, even ones made with a store-bought jelly roll and layered with readymade custard. There are everyday versions with nuts on top or canned peaches, and I have had fancy ones with spiced pears, rosewater and marsala ice cream—like this one, a combination that is pure paradise.

Serves 10

2 cups freshly brewed black coffee
¼ cup dry marsala
1 cup water
⅓ cup superfine sugar, plus 2 tablespoons extra
3 rhubarb stalks, cut into 4-inch lengths
3 egg yolks

1 pound mascarpone
1¼ cups cream
14–16 lady fingers
1 pint raspberries
1 pint blueberries
1 pint strawberries, hulled

Combine the coffee and marsala in a wide bowl and set aside to cool.

Put the water and ⅓ cup superfine sugar in a saucepan and heat gently until the sugar dissolves. Add the rhubarb and simmer for 15 minutes or until soft. Drain and leave to cool.

Put the egg yolks and 2 tablespoons sugar in a mixing bowl and beat with electric beaters for about 5 minutes, until light and creamy. Add the mascarpone and cream and beat until smooth.

Dip half the lady fingers in the coffee one at a time, until they are well moistened but not too soft, and arrange them in the bottom of a serving bowl or in individual parfait glasses.

Spread the rhubarb over the biscuits, then scatter over the raspberries. Spread half the mascarpone cream on top and scatter the blueberries over the cream.

Soak the remaining biscuits in coffee and lay them over the blueberries. Spread on the rest of the mascarpone. Arrange the strawberries on top.

Cover and refrigerate for at least 6 hours before serving, or even better overnight.

Extravagance
Generosity
Love
Tradition
Life
/ Food

*Extravagance, generosity, love, tradition, life, food.* These words mean so much to me; it is as if they are the very essence of who I am. Cooking is such a natural thing for me to do. Like painting, it allows me to escape from the rest of the world.

Extravagance is about the theater I bring to the modest spaces in which I live and work every day. It is about creating an environment for my family, staff and customers that will lift their spirits and bring an appreciation of all that is good in life. Generosity, flavored with love and seasoned with tradition, feeds my body, gives me joy and nourishes my soul.

Learning from parents and grandparents, I am like most people who love the experience of gathering ingredients, of preparing them well and enjoying them to the full. Life, and conversation, is a shared experience.

And where better to share that experience than at a barbecue on the beach? One I organized at Balnarring Beach on Victoria's Mornington Peninsula was a particularly lavish affair, the centerpiece being three large lobsters caught just twenty minutes before they were cooked. Like the recipes that follow, that barbecue was a true celebration of food.

It is beautiful out there on Westernport Bay. I love this part of the Peninsula best, away from all the development farther down the southern tip on Port Phillip Bay. There is an old-fashioned glamour here; life is slower, quieter and more truthful to its surroundings.

The barbecue was organized for guests from London. The aim was to give them the opportunity to experience something exotic, with an element of surprise that celebrated the local environment. And so live lobsters from Flinders Island were placed in a specially assembled holding pen some yards away from the shore. Wines and a selection of antipasti were served as the visitors watched their host, John Wrout, row out to collect the lobsters from the pen. It was a gorgeous autumn day, with just a slight salty breeze cooling the air. As John came to shore, his catch bouncing around in a big white bucket behind him, some cloud cover drifted over us. John lifted up a plump crustacean, tail flapping, to display its dimensions. There was less reflection from the water now so this beautiful creature, its jagged body hanging from John's fingers, seemed somehow all the more sacred in the dull light.

There was quite a discussion that day about the most humane way of killing a live lobster. Having not had a lot of experience, especially with such a fresh catch as these, I listened eagerly to the various suggestions. I had tried the method of freezing and then plunging into boiling water, but the creature had flapped about angrily in the boiling water while I'd held down the lid of the pot as hard as I could. Obviously, I had not kept the beast in the freezer long enough to put it to sleep.

John came up with what seemed to be the most humane method, and seeing as he had prepared and cooked lobster many times, I decided to take his advice. John felt the most sensible approach was to drown them in ice-cold fresh water. So I did just that. I filled a large bucket with some ice and fresh water, then plunged the lobster, headfirst, into the bucket. There was some flapping, but not for long.

Lobsters are beautiful creatures. We need to treat them with respect, both alive and on the plate, and prepare them in the simplest way.

# Yellowfin tuna carpaccio

A carpaccio is very thinly sliced meat or fish, usually served raw or just seared, accompanied by a simple dressing. Carpaccio was named by Giuseppe Cipriani of Harry's Bar in Venice in 1950, after the Italian Renaissance artist Vittore Carpaccio, who was a master of using combinations of brilliant reds and white.

Serves 12

⅓ cup olive oil, plus extra for frying
1 garlic clove, finely chopped
2 small red chilies, finely chopped
¼ teaspoon smoked paprika
large pinch of salt
four 10-ounce yellowfin tuna steaks

2 radishes
juice of 1½ lemons
½ bunch chives, cut into ¾-inch lengths
1 tablespoon small capers, rinsed

Put the ⅓ cup oil, garlic, chilies, paprika and salt on a large plate or dish and mix together. Wash the tuna steaks and pat them dry, then press each one into the mixture. Flip the steaks over and coat the other side. Leave to marinate for about 1 hour in the refrigerator.

Meanwhile, cut the radishes into fine matchsticks and put them in a small bowl. Add the juice of half a lemon and cover with a little water (this is to stop them browning).

When the tuna has marinated, heat a little extra oil in a frying pan until hot and sear each steak for about 20 seconds on each side. Set aside to cool a little, then cut the steaks into ⅓-inch strips and arrange the slices on a serving platter. Drizzle with the remaining lemon juice and scatter with the drained radish sticks, chives and capers, and serve.

# Lobster with spalmato duo

For this recipe, you can either boil or barbecue your lobster, and I have given instructions for both. The word *spalmato* sounds rather fancy, but it is simply what I have come up with in my search for a word that translates to "dip" in Italian. My coffee supplier suggested it. I love the way it sounds in my mouth, as I say it with the emphasis on the "o." As well as the two spalmatos, I serve this with a green salad of baby romaine, watercress, torn iceberg lettuce, shaved fennel and parsley.

Serves 12

EGGPLANT SPALMATO
2 large eggplants
4 garlic cloves, crushed
zest and juice of 1 lemon
⅓ cup olive oil
4 dill sprigs, finely chopped
salt and freshly ground black pepper

BELL PEPPER AND MACADAMIA SPALMATO
⅓ cup olive oil
1 onion, sliced
4 bell peppers, sliced
2 garlic cloves, crushed
1 cup macadamias, chopped
zest and juice of 1 lemon
½ cup natural yogurt

½ cup olive oil
zest and juice of 1 lemon
2 garlic cloves, crushed
1 small bunch parsley, finely chopped
salt and freshly ground black pepper
three 5½–6½-pound whole live lobsters

For the eggplant spalmato: heat the grill of a barbecue or a chargrill pan and add the eggplants. Cook, turning every so often, until the skin is charred and blistered all over (you can also do this in a hot oven). Remove from the heat and leave to cool a little, then peel away the skin and roughly chop the flesh.

Put the eggplant and remaining ingredients in a food processor and blend to a chunky purée. Taste for seasoning.

*Continued*
→

# Lobster with spalmato duo
## (continued)

For the bell pepper spalmato: heat the oil in a heavy-based frying pan and add the onion. Fry gently until translucent, then add the bell peppers and cook for 10–15 minutes until soft.

Transfer to a food processor along with the remaining ingredients and blend to a chunky purée. Taste for seasoning.

Combine the ½ cup oil, lemon zest and juice, garlic and parsley, season with salt and pepper in a bowl and set aside. Decide on whether to boil or barbecue the lobster, then either put a large pot of water on to boil or preheat a barbecue grill. While it is coming to the boil/heating, drown the lobsters by putting them in a large bucket of cold water. They will move around for a while, then stop, but you should leave them submerged for about 15 minutes.

To boil, plunge the lobsters into the pot of boiling water and boil for about 20 minutes (you may have to cook one or two at a time, depending on the size of your pot). Remove the lobsters from the pot and let them cool a little, then place them on a chopping board facing up. Split them down the middle through the head and tail using a sharp, heavy knife or, even better, a cleaver. You will need to use some force. Brush the exposed tail flesh with the parsley dressing and arrange the halves on a platter. I leave the legs attached so people can pull them off themselves. Serve straight away with the spalmato.

To barbecue, split the lobsters in half before cooking and brush the flesh with the parsley dressing. Place the halves on the barbecue, flesh-side down, then turn them over after around 5–10 minutes. Cook for another 10 minutes on the shell side, meanwhile painting the flesh with more dressing. Arrange on a platter and serve.

# Cauliflower soup

One of my favorite ways of serving soup is topped with a grilled slice of sourdough, sprinkled with grated grana padano and chopped herbs, and drizzled with extra-virgin olive oil. Whenever I make a soup it's never for two or four or six—who can be bothered? If you're going to prepare a soup, make a big batch of it; then you can freeze it or even use it in other dishes such as pasta. I use everyday pumpkin soup as a pasta sauce by adding a little to the cooked pasta along with ricotta or feta, and you could do this with cauliflower soup, too. Soup like this also works as a sauce for gnocchi.

Serves 12

½ cup olive oil

4 tablespoons butter

1 onion, finely chopped

1 carrot, finely chopped

1 celery stick, finely chopped

pinch of dried chili flakes (optional)

1 leek (white part only), finely sliced

2 garlic cloves, finely chopped

1 medium cauliflower, head cut into florets, stem skinned and cut into chunks

14-ounce can diced Italian tomatoes

3 quarts water

4–5 dill sprigs, leaves picked and chopped

salt and freshly ground black pepper

Heat the oil and butter in a large pot and gently fry the onion, carrot, celery and chili flakes (if using) until the onion is translucent. Add the leek and fry until it wilts, then add the garlic and cook for another 30 seconds. Add the cauliflower and tomatoes, raise the heat slightly and cover with a lid. Cook for 10–15 minutes, stirring occasionally, then add the water and simmer, partially covered, for about 1 hour.

Add the dill and blend the soup with a hand-held blender, keeping it a little chunky. Season with salt and pepper and serve.

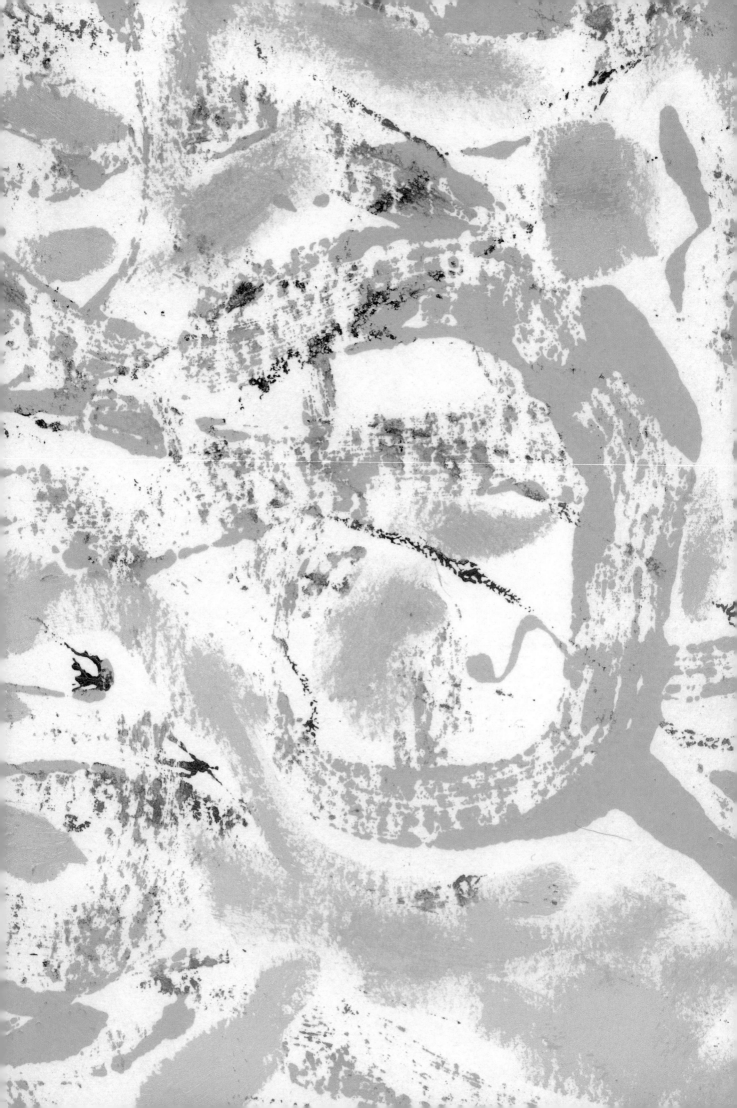

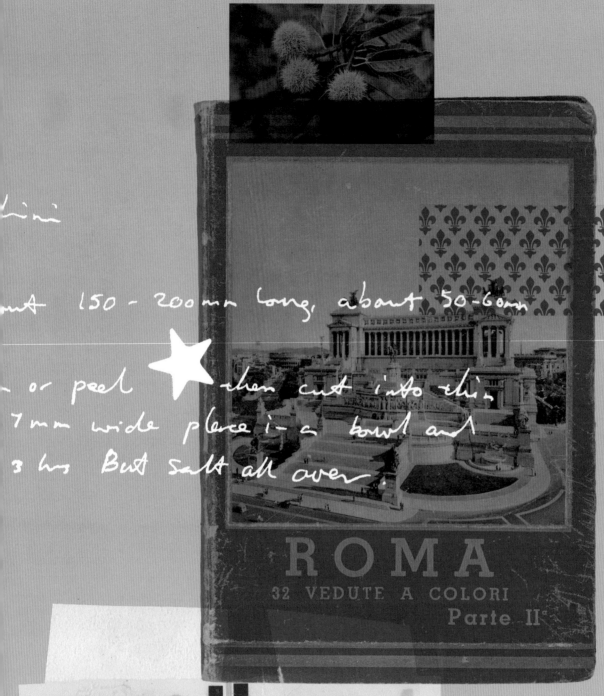

...ini

...ut 150 - 200mn long, about 50-60mn

... or peel ⭐ then cut into thin
...7mm wide piece in a bowl and
...3 hrs But salt all over.

ROMA
32 VEDUTE A COLORI
Parte II°

Come ti vidi mi innamorai./ E tu sorridi
perchè lo sai.
    When I saw you I fell in love./ And you
    smiled because you knew.
Je tombai amoureux de toi sitôt que je te
vis./ Et tu souris car tu le sais.
    En cuanto te vi me enamoré./ Y tu sonries
    porque lo sabes.
No momento em que te vi me apaixonei. E
você sorriu porque soube.
                    (Arrigo Boito)

il cuore non ha rughe.
    The heart has no wrinkles.
Le cœur n'a pas de rides.
    El corazón no tiene edad.
O coração não tem rugas.

                (M.se de Sévigné)

Postscript

I wasn't born in Sicily but my parents were. At the heart
of our cooking is the delight we take in wanting to please,
offering a warm welcome when we invite people to sit down
at our table and share our food.

When I am asked to choose the food that I love to cook
and eat—something I'm asked quite often—I have to take a
deep breath and think of the things that make me hungry.

The food that always springs to mind is pasta. I can't live
without it. I could quite happily prepare and eat a plate of
pasta every day of the week.

If I had a choice, rigatoni with *salsa di pomodoro* (classic
tomato sauce) would be my last meal on this earth. Take
4½ pounds of ripe roma tomatoes, wash them and cut them
into rough portions; it's up to you whether you include the
skin and seeds. In a heavy-based pan, cook a finely chopped
onion in 4 tablespoons of olive oil until translucent. Add
2 thinly sliced garlic cloves, stir and cook this gently for a
couple of minutes, then add the tomatoes, a handful of torn
basil leaves or some parsley. Cover and cook on a gentle to
medium heat until the sauce becomes a little thicker, which
should take about 30 minutes. Season with salt and pepper.
I also like to add a little sugar, as I find it tends to lighten
the sauce. You could also add a little butter at this stage to
intensify the flavor, say about half a cup. It gives the sauce
a lovely velvety quality.

Sometimes I use a blender to purée the sauce a little—it makes it less chunky—and while I am blending, I'll add some more fresh basil leaves. The sauce is now ready to mix through your favorite pasta. But be careful not to drown the pasta in the sauce; just use enough for the quantity of pasta you feel is necessary. Store the rest in the refrigerator or freezer, ready for another time. You could use this method to make a spicier sauce by adding chopped anchovies and whole small Sicilian capers to the onions and garlic, or perhaps some sliced fresh or dried red chilies.

I love this pasta when Johanne tops it with fried thinly sliced eggplant, served with freshly grated pecorino or grana padano, maybe spoonfuls of fresh ricotta and more shredded basil.

This reminds me of another favorite: chargrilled eggplant, simply prepared and piled onto garlicky, oily bruschetta. Huge white platters of it, scattered with fresh oregano and flat-leaf parsley.

Cut 2 eggplants into thick slices, sprinkle with a little salt and let stand in a colander for about half an hour. Pat dry with a paper towel. Brush the sides with olive oil and grill on a preheated grill until brown on both sides. Place on a large serving plate where you have already piled some grilled crusty bread that has been rubbed with fresh garlic, drizzled with olive oil and seasoned with salt and lots of freshly ground black pepper. Layer the eggplants, and sprinkle finely chopped garlic cloves and sprigs of oregano and flat-leaf parsley over the top of each layer. Squeeze on some lemon juice and season with salt and freshly ground pepper—what could be more healthful, more relaxed or more simple?

2.3.00 I love the expression that Paul achieves in his drawings – especially his trees – They are like these massive gentle giants – and his always looking up at them

Crostata

'Lets go to Rome to-night, and not come back'.
Hemingway - A farewell to arms

A GIRL
Horse

4 tablespoons olive oil.
eggs salt and freshly ground pepper
...d remove the outer leaves until you
...m around the edge. 2 Cut 2.5cm from
...ntion of the leaves. As you work, rub
...p them from discolouring. 3 Halve the
...ly into 4. 4 Place the artichokes into
... about 5-7 minutes or until tender.

I also love cheese—the strong, hard varieties as much as the tangy, creamy ones. Provolone or a soft young pecorino oozing over bread as it is grilling, topped with something a little different like walnuts or maybe freshly cut new season's sour peaches.

When I buy cheese, I like to bring it home in large blocks so we can cut chunks off it, either for grating onto pasta or risotto, or for enjoying with olives and some torn crusty bread and a glass of wine while preparing dinner. Pecorino and grana padano are my favorites. I grew up with the pecorino cheese that Mum and Dad would buy from Italian delicatessens on the other side of the city.

Plunge a spoon into soft mascarpone mixed with a little sugar, a squeeze of lemon juice and a few drops or more of Galliano. Toss in some ripe figs and chopped roasted hazelnuts, enjoy with an espresso and celebrate life.

Slice mozzarella and cover with the juice from freshly squeezed ripe cherry tomatoes. Toss together with olive oil, sliced garlic, some shredded basil leaves and glossy black olives.

Boil some broccolini until tender, then drain and dress it with olive oil and a little lemon juice. Spoon on ricotta and season with some salt and pepper, add shavings of parmigiano, thinly sliced chilies and sprigs of dill. Serve on a platter and drizzle with olive oil.

One of my wife's favorite pastas is drained spaghetti simply tossed gently with crumbled ricotta. She adores it and finds it perfectly satisfying with a glass of her favorite wine. Or, you can do as I do and drain just-cooked spaghetti, return it to the pot and add crumbled ricotta, some grated grana padano, freshly ground black pepper, whole roasted pine nuts, finely chopped garlic and sprigs of flat-leaf parsley. Toss them together with a little olive oil, just enough to be almost slippery. As Maggie Beer says, "A recipe is only a base, after all."

My stomach often needs refueling during the day. I am one of those people who need to "snack" regularly. I love bread, especially sourdough with its hard exterior and chewy interior. Panini spread with homemade mayonnaise and stuffed with mixed lettuce leaves, garlicky herbed chicken schnitzel and a squeeze of lemon. Or thick slices of grainy whole-wheat bread, spread with goat's cheese, filled with grated carrot, slices of Granny Smith apple, beet, frisée lettuce and some chopped walnuts. Full of rich flavors and color, and making the most of home-style baked bread. But sometimes you just have to have soft, perfectly square white bread wrapped around a chargrilled Aussie snag dripping with tomato sauce and some brown onions that have been caramelized on the hotplate. Bloody good!

Whenever Jo and I are away from home, the first thing I do is look around for a good-quality local baker. I can't live without my bread. It's the first thing I grab when I visit my parents. Dad always sits at the head of the table; I'm on his left and Mum sits opposite, but usually she is a blur, scurrying around her kitchen and always putting more plates on the table. Their homemade olives, cheeses and cured meats, fennel from the garden and a frittata or two. I love it. I love their generosity and humor and the conversations we have.

And in the morning? Sometimes I have cake for breakfast. Plunger coffee, a newspaper and a piece of cake. Don't ask me to choose what flavor; they all tempt me. It's a great way to start the day, indulgent and special, and removes any hint of a dull day unfolding. A mixed berry cake sounds thoroughly healthful, especially when made with yogurt and just a little butter.

Get up early, and grease and line a 9-inch round springform cake pan with parchment paper. In a bowl, combine 3 cups of self-rising flour and 2 cups of mixed berries (frozen or fresh), making sure you mix the berries through the flour. Add 2 cups of superfine sugar, 3 eggs, 1 cup of milk, 1 cup of yogurt, 5 tablespoons of butter, 1 teaspoon of cinnamon, the zest of 1 orange and stir the lot until just combined. Pour into the prepared pan and bake in a preheated 350°F oven for about 1 hour.

Now go for a one-hour walk while it cooks. When you get home, remove the cake from the pan when it has cooled slightly, then sit down and enjoy the most delicious and decadent breakfast. Why wait all day for dessert?

I end this book by encouraging you not to follow my recipes. Change them; be creative, be different. Have fun in the kitchen. *Eat Ate* is about belonging, but it is also about having an alternative point of view. When you are cooking, think of extravagance, generosity, tradition, life and love. And food.

one eye sees,
the other feels    Paul Klee

# Index

## Acknowledgments

Thank you, Johanne, for every moment. The best journey is coming home to you every night. To our children, Danielle, Pam and Paul, thank you for looking after me and keeping the old man in line. You are all strong, intelligent, confident people and I adore each of you.

My parents, Diego and Pina, for teaching me about extravagance, generosity, love, tradition, life and food. I am so fortunate that I was born to you and grew up in a Sicilian environment at home.

My sister Rosa, a passionate woman, and her husband Michael, to whom I am so grateful. When their children, Sophie and the twins Francesca and Marcella, come into the café all hell breaks loose. I love it!

To my sister Josie and her husband Pino, thank you for teaching me the art of being calm when dealing with customers. To Daniel and Jessica, you rock. I love your individualism. To my brother Frank and his wife Jenny and their sons, Richard and Robert. Frank, no brothers could be more opposite but at the same time similar family men and with businesses revolving around food. I love our conversations about staff, banks and customers.

To all our customers at Shop Ate, I love cooking and serving you. You keep the passion alive in me.

Thank you to all our suppliers, Kevin our butcher, Village Fruits, Paul and Reece our bakers, Graham our milkman, the effervescent Anna our poultry lady, Rosemary, Graham and Kim our egg people, Genovese Coffee for the best coffee beans in the world. Bruno for all our dry goods. To the winemakers, Trent at Five Sons Estate, Arthur O'Brian Stonier Wines, and Gary Crittenden whose passion for just about everything is infectious.

To Earl Carter, what you do with light is remarkable, challenging and original. To Caroline Velik, thank you for being such an understanding food stylist with such elegant restraint.

To the makers of this book, Sandy Grant and Julie Pinkham for your faith in the project. Mary Small, you have such a great eye and enthusiasm for the way you marshalled your team into action. To Rachel Pitts and Janet Austin, thank you for checking that the words made sense. To Ellie Smith for the final detail and wrapping the book to its final destination to the printer, thank you for your good taste.

My dear friend, Dominic Hofstede, steered the design through some tricky patches. I trusted your judgment from the beginning. You have captured the beauty. I thank you.

And finally to my dear staff, what can I say, you inspire me every day. You are all remarkable men and women. Brigid Hardstone, Chris Jager, Christopher McLeay, Jenn Neff, Naterlie Nowotarski, Patrick Williams, Debbie Savin, Pam and Paul Mirabella and Rosa Malignaggi. All of you make Shop Ate. Thank you.

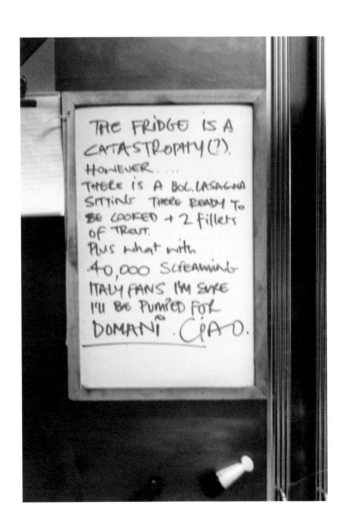